CHARLEMAGNE

Matthias Becher

translated by David S. Bachrach

Yale University Press

New Haven and London

Designed by Adam Freudenheim
Set by Alliance Interactive Technology in Sabon and Albertus MT
Printed in the USA

Library of Congress Cataloging-in-Publication Data
Becher, Mathias.
    [Karl der Grosse. English]
    Charlemagne / by Matthias Becher; translated by David S. Bachrach.
        p. cm.
    "Originally published in a slightly different form as Karl der Grosse,
1999, by C.H. Beck, Munich"—T.p. verso.
    Includes bibliographical references and index.
        ISBN 0-300-09796-4 (cloth)
        ISBN 978-0-300-10758-6 (paper)
        1. Charlemagne, Emperor, 742–814. 2. France—Kings and
rulers—Biography. 3. Holy Roman Empire—Kings and rulers—Biography.
4. France—History—To 987. 5. Holy Roman Empire—History—To 1517.
I. Title
        DC73.B39 2003
        944'.014'092—dc21
                                            2003007858

A catalogue record for this book is available from the British Library

Sandwell
Metropolitan Borough Council

Please return this item to any Sandwell Library on or before the return date.

You may renew the item unless it has been reserved by another borrower.

You can renew your library items by using the 24/7 renewal hotline number - ~~0845 352 4949~~ or FREE online at opac-lib.sandwell.gov.uk

THANK YOU FOR USING YOUR LIBRARY GB

20/7/17		

I2796379

Contents

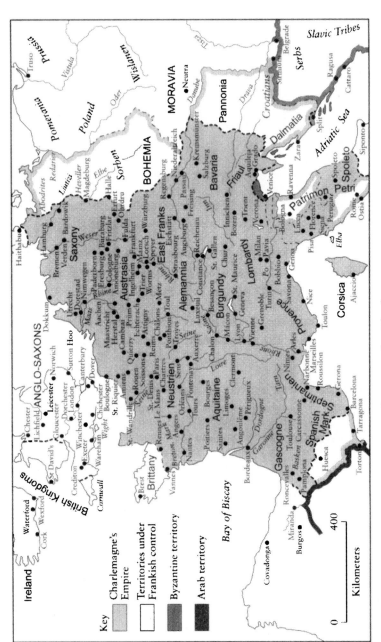

Europe under Charlemagne

Introduction

More so than any other medieval ruler, Charlemagne is well known, even today, to a wider public. His very person is inextricably bound to the idea of historical greatness. In several European languages, his name and his epithet have become tied inseparably together as *Charlemagne* or *Carlomagno*. There can be no doubt that he was an important ruler. However, does this relate to his personality? What do we know about the character and the human qualities of the "great Charles"? In comparison to other medieval rulers, the sources available to answer this question are rather substantial. We have an almost contemporary description of Charlemagne's life from the pen of one of his trusted intimates. The broadly educated Einhard, who was born into an East Frankish noble family, came to Charlemagne's court at the end of the eighth century and quickly made his career there. He composed his *Vita Karoli magni* about ten years after the death of the emperor. In general, a medieval observer of a monarch

1

confined himself to portraying him as the ideal ruler who embodied a universally accepted catalogue of Christian virtues. By contrast, the individual character of the ruler was unimportant. Einhard, however, refrained from stressing these Christian virtues, and emphasized instead other general and unchanging characteristics. Thus, for example, Charlemagne exceeded, "all the other rulers of his time in both wisdom and generosity of spirit." Einhard's detailed descriptions of the emperor's private and family life are introduced by a reference to his steadfastness in the face of both fortune and adversity. He bore the enmity of the Byzantine emperor with patience and generosity of spirit. Indeed, Einhard offers an exceptionally vivid image of Charlemagne:

> He was broad and strong in the form of his body and exceptionally tall without, however, exceeding an appropriate measure. As is well known, his height was equal to the length of seven of his feet. The top of his head was round, his eyes were very large and lively. His nose was somewhat larger than was usual. He had attractive gray hair, and a friendly, cheerful face. His appearance was impressive whether he was sitting or standing despite having a neck that was fat and too short, and a large belly. The symmetry of his other limbs obscured these points. He had a firm gait, a thoroughly manly manner of holding himself, and a high voice which did not really correspond to the rest of his body. He was healthy aside from the four years before he died when he frequently suffered from fever, and finally also developed a limp. Even at this time, however, he followed his own counsel rather than the advice of the doctors, whom he very nearly hated, because they advised him

to give up roasted meat, which he loved, and to restrict himself to boiled meat instead. He regularly rode and hunted, as was the custom of his people. . . . He greatly enjoyed the steam from the warm springs. He was a very practiced swimmer and enjoyed it so much that it was very difficult to get him to leave. It is for this reason that he built a royal palace at Aachen and lived there regularly during the last years of his life. He invited not only his sons, but also the nobles, his friends, and frequently his men and his bodyguards to join him in the baths so that at times a hundred or more men were bathing with him.

The crowd may not have been that large since Einhard was inclined to exaggerate, often to the benefit of his hero whom he idealized. In his descriptions, Einhard frequently borrowed from the *vitae*, the biographies of the Roman emperors, composed by the classical author Suetonius. As a consequence, Einhard invented only a few details independently. His description of the size of Charlemagne's body, however, has been confirmed, to a certain extent, by measurements of his skeleton. The emperor was actually over 1.8 m. in height, which corresponds to seven feet. He did at least mention several of the great ruler's minor external flaws: his large nose, his short neck, his hanging belly, and his high-thin voice. Consequently, it may be possible to believe some of the other information as well. Our source did not treat the ruler's character as an independent subject. Nevertheless, his description permits one to imagine certain weaknesses—stubbornness, an inclination to gluttony, and the need always to be at the center of a large group. This is mirrored in Einhard's claim that Charlemagne made friends very easily and was a frank and open man. His love of good eating must have made quite an impression since Einhard stressed the emperor's appetite on another occasion: "He could not be moderate in eating, indeed, he frequently complained that fasting weakened the body." However, he always detested drunkenness, not only in himself, but in others as well.

Other personal characteristics were allowed to shine through as, for example, Charlemagne's talkativeness: "The words flowed richly from his mouth, and he could easily and clearly express what he wanted. . . . He was so eloquent that it could even seem like he was prattling." The extroverted nature of his personality was most obvious on sad occasions. At the death of his sons and his daughter, Charlemagne "bore up with less composure than one might have expected given the greatness of his spirit. He had enormous paternal love, and he shed many tears. Also, when he heard about the death of the Roman pope Hadrian, whom he had loved most among all of his friends, he cried as much as if he had lost a brother or his most beloved son." He loved his daughters so much that he did not permit them to marry. We get an image of a gregarious patriarch who could also be modest in his personal affairs. Thus, Charlemagne only held large banquets on high feast days, almost always wore simple clothing, and wore gowns or foreign robes only on festive occasions.

In addition, Einhard stressed that Charlemagne followed an irregular pattern in his life which strongly resembled that of the first Roman emperor Augustus: while in summer, he slept two to three hours after the midday meal, during the night he interrupted his sleep, "four or five times and not only woke up, but also got up. While he was putting on his clothing and his shoes, he summoned not only his friends, but if the count of the palace had mentioned a lawsuit that could not be decided without consulting him, he immediately summoned the litigants and gave a judgment after hearing the case, as if he was sitting on the bench. This was not the only thing he did during those hours. He saw to what business had to be done that day and assigned tasks to one of his servants in the same hour." Charlemagne also supposedly spent these nights practicing his writing, although without much success. During the Middle Ages, writing and reading were not inextricably linked, so Charlemagne's ability to read remains a controversial issue. His thirst for knowledge, however, drove him to concern himself with the sciences of his day. He was even interested in astronomy and the passage of the stars. In addition, at mealtimes, he had the works of Saint Augustine read to him. However, it remains an open question how deeply he engaged with higher learning. After all, according to Einhard, the mealtime readings included "the histories and deeds of times past" and music was also played at these times. Presumably, such entertainments meant more to the ruler than erudite treatises.

Despite the impressive description of his appearance and some of his characteristics, it is not possible to write a biography of Charlemagne that satisfies modern demands. Einhard's portrayal is too dependent on certain stereotypes. In addition, we lack personal documents which could give information about Charlemagne's thoughts and feelings. We only have sources that describe in more or less detail his actions and thereby permit a political biography. However, even with this more limited ambition, the modern historian soon reaches his limits. Most of the sources are silent about his motives. As a consequence, it is not possible to give an unambiguous answer on the matter of his success. Clearly, the conquest of Saxony was a victory for the Frankish kingdom. Was it, however, a success in view of the victims and in view of the fact that Charlemagne required about thirty years to bring it about? Thus, this little volume is, as is the case with other modern biographies of early and high medieval rulers, an individual interpretation based on years of engagement with the sources and the scholarly literature.

I

THE HIGHPOINT OF HIS REIGN

The Imperial Coronation of Charlemagne on Christmas Day in the Year 800

The feast of the birth of Jesus in the year 800: on the morning of Christmas Day, Charlemagne entered the church of St. Peter in Rome in order to participate in the third Christmas mass that, according to longstanding custom, was to be celebrated by the pope. Laying prostrate, they prayed the *oratio*. Then, as Charlemagne rose, Leo III took a crown and placed it on the head of the Frankish king. The Romans who were present immediately understood the significance of this act. They appealed to the saints and acclaimed Charlemagne as emperor calling out three times: *Carolo piisimo augusto, a Deo coronato magno et pacifico imperatore* [*sic*], *vita et victoria!*—"To Charles the most pious Augustus, crowned by God, the great and pacific emperor, life and victory!" According to longstanding tradition, the pope honored the new emperor by prostrating himself at his feet.

The events of Christmas Day 800 were spectacular and were to have far-reaching consequences. This moment witnessed the founding of the medieval empire that would later continue as the Holy Roman Empire of the German Nation until 1806. At the same time, this empire was bound closely to the papacy, although Charlemagne had not intended this to be the case. Contemporaries were certainly aware of the importance of this act. Charlemagne challenged the Byzantine Empire, which considered itself to be continuing the old *Imperium Romanum* without interruption. Up to this point, the east Roman emperor residing in Constantinople had also been recognized in western Europe as the holder of the highest secular office. No Frankish, Lombard, or Gothic king had ever seriously contested this leading position. Until Leo III's predecessor Hadrian, the popes had also seen the emperor as their most important partner in theological matters, while the Frankish king was to take over the secular protection of the pope and the city of Rome. Without the imperial title, Charlemagne remained in the second rank, despite all his actual power, and he had to stand back behind the highest representatives of spiritual and temporal power, the pope and the emperor in the East.

Upheaval in the eternal city set in motion a series of developments which ultimately led to Charlemagne's imperial coronation. Pope Hadrian died in 795. In contrast to his predecessor, Leo III owed his elevation to his long service in the Roman Church and was not a member of one of the leading noble families in the city of Rome. Very soon, tensions arose between the new pope and the aristocracy. The contemporary sources do not make clear the nature of these tensions but one might guess that they were due to the division of power and influence inside the city of Rome and in its surrounding territories. Those most dissatisfied were Paschalis, a nephew of Hadrian, and Campulus. Both of them were high officials in the papal administration and had served under Hadrian. The rebels used the occasion of a procession on the feast of Saint Mark (25 April) to stage a coup. The pope was seized and mistreated. Some even intended to blind him and cut out his tongue. Such mistreatment had the intended effect of making the victim unfit for office over the long term. In fact, the pope was subjected to a formal process of deposition in the church at the monastery of San Silvestro in Capite. He was locked up there and later transferred to the monastery of San Erasmo in Monte Celio.

However, the conspirators did not dare to elevate a new pope before approaching the Frankish king Charlemagne, who controlled upper and central Italy. After all, he had formally recognized Leo, who, on the occasion of his election, had sent him the keys to the tomb of Saint Peter and the banner of the city of Rome thereby publicly confirming Charlemagne's role as the protector of Rome. The rebels could not ignore him if they hoped to succeed in their efforts. Paschalis and Campulus did not to have to fear these necessary consultations. Because of their close relationship with Pope Hadrian, whom Charlemagne had greatly esteemed, they were part of a group that was well-liked at the Frankish court. Indeed Frankish ambassadors appeared in the eternal city in the early summer. Admittedly, further events did not develop as the conspirators had hoped. Some tensions probably arose between them and Charlemagne's representatives, whose presence, and perhaps even whose direct intervention, made Leo's release possible. The situation became so complicated that only Charlemagne could make a final decision. The pope and perhaps a delegation of his opponents as well were therefore escorted north to the Frankish court in order to defend their respective positions.

Despite news of the coup, King Charlemagne had not given

up his plans for a campaign against Saxony set for 799, although he had been planning to make an appearance in Rome. Instead, he moved from Aachen, crossed the Rhine, and spent the summer at his palace at Paderborn, while his son Charles went on toward the Elbe and campaigned against the rebel Saxons. While the pope and his enemies were en route, the Frankish court discussed further action, as we learn from the letters of Alcuin, the head of Charlemagne's court school. Alcuin adopted a rule of law from the notorious "forgeries of Symmachus," written in the early sixth century: *Prima sedes a nemine iudicatur,* "the first seat [meaning the pope] is not to be judged by anyone." At times, however, there was considerable debate at the royal court as to whether Leo should remain pope. Plaintiffs, who were probably emissaries of the Roman conspirators, came forward and charged Leo with adultery and perjury. The charges were so grave and explosive that Alcuin burned a letter dealing with them, "so that no offense could be taken because of carelessness by the keeper of the letter." Finally, however, the "defenders" of the pope succeeded. In addition, it would seem reasonable to assume that Leo did everything in his power to win Charlemagne over to his side. On offer—the empire.

At the end of the eighth century, a document known as the *Constitutum Constantini,* or so-called donation of Constantine, was produced at the papal court. According to legend, out of gratitude for his cure from leprosy, the Roman emperor Constantine the Great (306–337) is supposed to have made the following concessions to the Roman bishop Silvester: he recognized the primacy of Rome over every church, he bestowed the imperial emblems on the head of the Roman church, and he granted him not only the city of Rome, but also Italy and the remaining western provinces. Afterward, the emperor moved to the city on the Bosporus

that was named after him and contented himself with rule in the
East. If the pope actually shared these ideas, then it was no great
step to conclude that he had the right to a say in awarding the
empire. Charlemagne would not have immediately rejected this
position, since his father Pippin had already turned to Rome when
he wished to overthrow his Merovingian predecessor in order to
assume the kingship for himself. Even if Pippin and Charlemagne only followed the pope's will when it seemed politically
opportune, and otherwise ruled their kingdom and its churches
autocratically, the successors of Saint Peter were always appreci-
ated when it came to legitimate new offices. After all, the pope
was largely limited to his great spiritual reputation and therefore
posed no danger to the actual power of the Carolingians.

At Rome, Leo himself symbolically demonstrated his turn
towards the Frankish court. It was probably at this time that he
had the *triclinium* of the Lateran, the most important of the
papal audience chambers, decorated with remarkable mosaics.
The apse held an image of the dispatch of the apostles by Christ.
The wall to the left presumably showed the enthroned Christ.
He was granting the *pallium* (a stole) as a sign of office to Saint
Peter who was kneeling on his right side, and a *labarum* (the imperial standard) to Constantine the Great, who was kneeling on
his left. The corresponding right side of the apse showed the
image of an enthroned Saint Peter, who was handing the *pallium* to Pope Leo, and a *vexillum*, a standard, to King Charlemagne. The inscription beneath read: "Saint Peter gives life to
Pope Leo and victory to King Charles." Peter Classen explained
the mosaics in the following manner:

Here, just as between the pope and Saint Peter, so a paral-
lel is drawn between the Frankish king with his crown and

sword and Constantine, the founder of the Christian empire. Thus, he is portrayed as receiving the symbols of secular protection from Saint Peter. This was not an expression of sovereignty, but rather a proclamation that the protection—that is the direct protection of the Roman church, the pope, and the city of Rome, which originated in God and Saint Peter—had been assigned not to the successors of Constantine in the East but rather to the king of the Franks . . . Through this image Rome demonstrated very clearly that it had turned from Constantinople toward the Franks, and that Charlemagne had taken the place of Constantine.

However, subsequent events were to show where the real power lay. Instead of immediately quashing the charges against the pope, Charlemagne handled them as a kind of bargaining chip. Admittedly, a large number of Frankish bishops escorted the pope back to Rome in the fall of 799 and led an investigation—notably, this took place at the *triclinium* at the Lateran; however, from the point of view of the pope, the result was disappointing. The charges against him were not, in the end, dismissed, and the conspirators were merely sent into exile in Francia. Just as he had been before, Leo was still dependent on the sympathy and help of Charlemagne.

Charlemagne himself returned to Aachen from Paderborn. In early 800, he saw off an embassy from the patriarch of Jerusalem, which had brought him relics from the Holy Sepulcher. He sent along the priest Zacharias, who appeared in Rome shortly before the imperial coronation where he reported to his king. Thus, it is possible that Zacharias knew before setting out on his journey that Charlemagne would be at Rome at the end of the year. Furthermore, Charlemagne's activities over the course of the year 800 indicate that he was pursuing important goals. Early in the year, he toured his kingdom. At Tours, he not only met with Alcuin, but also had a kind of family conference with his three sons, Charles, Pippin, and Louis. The anonymous biographer of Louis stated expressly that this meeting served to plan the expedition to Italy.

A small delay may have resulted from the death of Charlemagne's wife Liutgard at Tours on June fourth. At the beginning of August, Charlemagne held an assembly at Mainz and then set out for Italy. When he reached Ravenna, Charlemagne paused for seven days. He sent his son Pippin to raid the independent principality of Benevento. He himself set out for Rome and was received solemnly by the pope and the Romans at Mentana, twelve miles from the city on November 23rd. After sharing a meal, the pope returned to Rome, and sent the banners of the city to the king for his entry on the next day. He organized "groups of foreigners and citizens to take up their positions in the appropriate places," who were to greet Charlemagne with songs of praise. Meanwhile, along with the clergy and bishops, he would make Charlemagne welcome on the steps of St. Peter's. This ceremony was already worthy of an emperor since the pope generally met the emperor six miles from the city, and in this case he met him at the twelfth mile. In his role as *patricius Romanorum*, the protector of Rome, Charlemagne had been greeted until now at the first milestone from Rome, and not by the pope himself. This change and its meaning must have been clear to all of the participants.

Indeed, Charlemagne was not only greeted like an emperor, even before his coronation he also acted like the highest secular authority in the world. A week after his arrival, he summoned the current ecclesiastical and secular magnates to a synod that took place at the pope's seat in the old imperial city of Rome. The most important business dealt with by the council was also worthy of an emperor. The assembly considered the charges against Pope Leo III which—perhaps according to Charlemagne's wishes—had not yet been dismissed.

These hearings went on for several weeks. Apparently, the assembled magnates from the Frankish kingdom and Rome could not solve the most important problem, namely the dismissal of the charges brought against the pope. No one wished to prove the validity of the charges, or to stand against him as an accuser. On the other hand, however, these charges had to be refuted in order to re-establish peace in Rome. Finally, Pope Leo deigned to purge himself through an oath. On 23 December, he mounted to the *ambo*, the pulpit, and holding up the gospels, he declared solemnly that he was not guilty of the charges brought against him. In this manner, the charges against him were quashed, because, in the eyes of his contemporaries, an oath of this type, sworn in a correct manner and without formal error, proved without doubt the truth of the speaker's words. The assembly was so relieved that a thanksgiving service was immediately held. However, there was no effort to turn attention toward the Roman conspirators whose charges had been proved false by Leo's oath. Instead, the assembly turned to another matter.

According to the *Annals* from the important monastery of Lorsch, after the pope's oath of purgation, the council, with the pope as its spokesman, decided "that Charles, the king of the Franks, had to be called emperor." The annalist offered a revealing description of the reasoning behind this decision. First, the *nomen imperatoris*, the imperial name or title, was vacant among the Byzantines because a woman had ruled there since 797. By contrast, God had "placed under Charles' authority Rome, where the Caesars had always been accustomed to reside, as well as the remaining imperial residences in Italy, Gaul, and Germania." Charlemagne could not ignore the requests of the assembly, and on Christmas Day he was anointed and received the imperial title from the pope. The *Annals* of Lorsch were the only contemporary account to deal with the political consequences of the imperial elevation, which was a challenge to the Byzantine empire. By calling into question Irene's ability to rule because of her sex, the Franks and the Romans established the rhetorical basis for Charlemagne's elevation as emperor. By referring to the *nomen imperatoris*, the author endorsed a traditional, widespread argument that can be traced back to the church fathers Augustine (354–430), and Isidore of Seville (560–636). Modern scholars refer to this type of argument as name-theory. According to this argument, a ruler had to fulfill the duties associated with his title, if he wished to bear this title or this name justly. If he did not, then this justified his replacement by a new king or emperor. In the same vein, the *Annals* stressed the fact that Charlemagne ruled large parts of the erstwhile Roman empire and therefore was the true successor of the ancient Caesars.

A further reason, which the annalist only mentioned as a consequence of the imperial coronation, was the settlement of the disagreements within the Roman church. Here, he meant the rebellion against the pope. Even if Charlemagne as king and *patricius* had already had the power to take legal action against the conspirators, as emperor he had the undoubted justification for undertaking this action. The rather inexact remarks of the Lorsch annalists are set in more concrete terms by the other sources. A few days after his elevation to emperor, Charlemagne summoned the conspirators to court and condemned them to death according to the provisions of Roman law. The pope interceded on their behalf, and succeeded in having them pardoned and only sent into exile. This, in any case, was the official Frankish version, while the papal accounts are silent on the subject of the pope's intervention. It is possible that only the Franks had an interest in their pardon. Perhaps Paschalis and Campulus were to be spared because of their relationships with Pope Hadrian, whom Charlemagne had cherished. In any event, they survived their Frankish exile safe and sound, and were able to return to Rome after Leo's death in 816.

There is a great deal of evidence to suggest that Charlemagne himself was the driving force behind his elevation as emperor. However, on the other side there is the evidence in Einhard's account of his life: "He went to Rome and spent the entire winter there in order to rescue the church from the great ruin which had befallen it. It was at this time that he acquired the title emperor and Augustus. At first, he was so opposed to this that he claimed he would never have entered the church on that day, despite the fact that it was a high feast, if he had known in advance the pope's intent." Admittedly, Einhard was writing almost a generation after the event. Many developments in the period after 800 may have led him to this assessment. Furthermore, it is possible that Einhard, who was shaped by the classical educational ideal, attributed a behavioral pattern to his hero which was drawn from his rhetorical lessons, and from the classical model image of the Roman emperors: public gestures of modesty and the implied rejection of the imperial honor. Perhaps Einhard simply felt obliged to try in retrospect to compensate for a perceived deficiency in his hero. In any case,

The Highpoint of His Reign

Charlemagne remained uncertain for a long time about what the name for the empire should be in future. From May 801, Charlemagne bore a title which accommodated the claims of his most important peoples: *Karolus serenissimus augustus a Deo coronatus magnus, pacificus imperator, Romanum gubernans imperium, qui et per misericordiam Dei rex Francorum atque Langobardorum,* "Charles, the most merciful, awe-inspiring, great, and pacific emperor crowned by God, who rules the Roman empire and who [is] king of the Franks and Lombards by the grace of God."

The attack on the pope in the summer of 799 accelerated Charlemagne's rise to the imperial dignity. Yet, even without the opportunity provided by the weakness of the papacy, he would probably have sought an enhancement of his status in relation to the old, east Roman empire. However that may be, the imperial dignity served as a symbolic bond for his enormous empire, which he had expanded through numerous wars into the largest empire in western Europe since the days of the *Imperium Romanum.* Whether these campaigns in the present states of Italy, Spain, Germany, Austria, and Hungary, were actually intended to achieve some overarching goal must remain unresolved given the lack of evidence in the sources concerning his intentions. His internal policies, which were intended to strengthen the position of the ruler, may be understood to have been influenced by the model of the erstwhile Roman empire, as well as of its eastern successor. Whatever its circumstances, however, the imperial coronation on Christmas Day in the year 800 symbolizes the high point not only of his reign, but also of the entire course of Frankish history.

II

FROM THE FALL OF THE ROMAN EMPIRE IN THE WEST TO CHARLEMAGNE'S ACCESSION TO POWER IN 768

A Short History of the Kingdom of the Franks

When Charlemagne came to power in 768, the kingdom of the Franks was already the most important power in Europe. Three centuries earlier in 476, however, when the Roman empire in western Europe collapsed, no one could have guessed that it would be the kingdom of the Franks that would step forward as its heir. This development came to fruition at Charlemagne's imperial coronation. This step had been heralded long before as the kingdom of the Franks had been the foremost power in the territory of the erstwhile *Imperium Romanum* since the second half of the sixth century. Nevertheless, in hindsight, the path which finally established the Franks as the heirs of Rome was marked by many setbacks.

The Franks received mention in Roman sources from the middle of the third century in the context of the great Germanic invasions which rocked the *Imperium Romanum* between the fifties and seventies of the third century. The name "Frank" which probably meant "brave, bold, and impetuous," was very likely a collective name given by outsiders to a mixed group of peoples living between the Rhine and Weser rivers. Warbands drawn from these peoples forced their way into the Roman empire in order to obtain booty and gain military acclaim. These bands were either destroyed by the Romans or settled as military colonists (*laeti*), mainly in the north of Gaul. Some of these Franks were also recruited to serve as soldiers in the Roman army. Increasingly after the middle of the fourth century, Franks and other Germanic groups were employed to carry out specific duties in Gaul and were transformed into subjects of the *Imperium* with military obligations.

The integration of the Franks into the *Imperium Romanum* went so far that many of them achieved high rank in the imperial army. The collapse of Roman imperial power in Gaul after the mid-fourth century provided the Franks with the opportunity to expand throughout much of northern Gaul. Cologne and Trier fell into their hands. One of the Frankish tribes, under the leadership of King Chlodio, conquered the area around Cambrai and pushed on toward the Somme. According to later, fabulous accounts, the series of Merovingian kings began with Chlodio, or rather with his son Merovech, who traced their ancestry back to the gods. In addition, the early Merovingians, like other Germanic kings, acted as the representatives of Roman imperial authority and thereby legitimized their rule in the eyes of the Gallo-Roman population.

In 482, Merovech's grandson Clovis appeared on the political stage. He conquered the remaining Roman possessions in northern Gaul, which were centered on Soissons. With this victory, the remaining elements of the imperial government fell into his hands, namely the fiscal lands, coinage, the tax administration, and even more importantly, the remainder of the imperial army including the arms factories and garrisons. In 496/97, Clovis made an exceptionally momentous decision to break with the pagan traditions of his ancestors and become Christian. He chose the Catholic form of this new religion, which was followed by the Gallo-Roman population, and was baptized at Rheims in 498. In this manner, Clovis surmounted the most important prerequisite for merging together his Franks with the Romans who constituted the vast majority of the population in his kingdom. In this respect, the kingdom of the Franks under Clovis differed decisively from the other large Germanic kingdoms that had been established in the territory of the erstwhile empire. The Goths, Burgundians, and Vandals also had become Christians. Initially, however, they followed the Arian rather than the Catholic doctrine. Because of his conversion to Christianity, Clovis was soon hailed as a "new Constantine." In the end, Clovis' decision to become a Catholic Christian proved to be decisive for the development of Frankish power in the territory of the erstwhile Roman empire at the expense of the other Germanic kingdoms.

During the final years of his reign, Clovis expanded his kingdom and decisively defeated the Alemmani no later than 506. Frankish influence at this point reached from the far bank of the Rhine to the Danube. In 507, Clovis defeated the Visigoths under their king Alaric II near Vouillé, in the region of Poitiers, and a year later captured the Visigothic capital of Toulouse. During this period Clovis probably also completed his elimination of the remaining Frankish (petty) kings. Thus he became king of all Franks. News of his successes reached as far as Constantinople. The East Roman emperor Anastasius I sanctioned Clovis' rule. In 508, Anastasius granted an honorary consulship to Clovis and transmitted to him the insignia of the royal office,

The Merovingian Dynasty

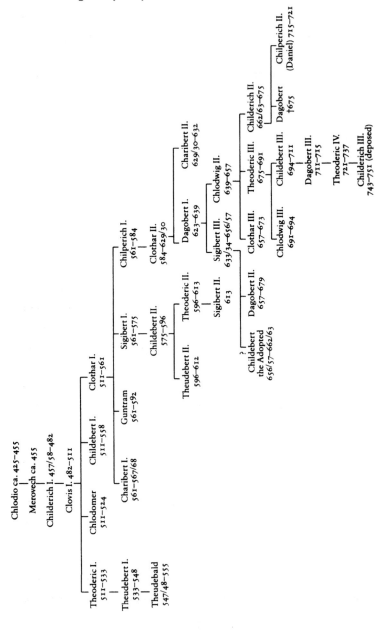

namely a purple tunic, a cloak, and diadem. This recognition set Clovis' manner of ruling within an imperial context. He copied the Roman emperor by presenting himself as a lawgiver, and at the end of his reign issued the laws of his people, which formerly had been transmitted orally, as a written code, the *Lex Salica*. In this tradition, he also held the first Frankish episcopal council which took place at Orléans in 511. This council saw the first close cooperation between the Frankish king and the highest level of Roman society, namely the bishops of Gaul.

Clovis died in 511 at the age of about 46. His kingdom, which stretched from the Rhine to the Pyrenees was divided among his four sons. One of them died just a few years later so that the kingdom was redivided among the three surviving sons. At first, the Frankish conquests went forward. Around 530, they conquered the kingdom of the Thuringians. In 532, they defeated the Burgundians. Two years later this kingdom too was divided among Clovis' sons. In 537, the Ostrogoths, who were being attacked by the Byzantines, withdrew from Provence and thereby purchased Frankish military assistance. In this manner, the Franks obtained enduring access to the Mediterranean, which was the central commercial zone of this period. These successes served to reinforce Frankish self-confidence. Theudebert (died 548), a grandson of Clovis, imitated the imperial system of government and intervened frequently in Italy after 539. North of the Alps, he expanded his kingdom up to Pannonia. He proudly pointed out these successes to the east Roman emperor Justinian (527–565) who was only able to conquer Italy after decades of campaigning.

This external demonstration of power corresponded to the internal status of the Merovingian kings. Their personal power was based above all on their ability to maintain a large military following whose members had sworn service and loyalty to them. In addition, the kings stood as guarantors of the legal order and of both internal and external peace. Thus, several of Clovis' successors presented themselves as lawgivers and expanded the *Lex Salica* through the addition of numerous titles. Because of the large numbers of Gallo-Romans living there, the remaining elements of the Roman administrative system were of central importance to the Merovingians in ruling their kingdoms. The material basis for their rule was based on the enormous land resources of the former Roman fisc. They had inherited these from the Roman emperor and his high officials. The Merovingian kings collected Roman taxes and tolls across wide areas of Gaul from which they obtained large sums of money.

The center of government of the kingdom was the royal court which also was organized on a Roman pattern. The office holders bore the title *comes*. Thus, for example, the *comes stabuli* was responsible for overseeing all transportation resources. In addition, there was the office of the *thesaurarius*, the treasurer, and the *cubicularius*, the chamberlain. The royal chancery was run by clerks who, as needed, could also take on wider responsibilities. The final office worth mentioning is that of the *maior domus*, i.e. the head of the household. As the name suggests, this officer originally was in charge of the royal house. In the second half of the sixth century, however, these officials gained considerable power as underage children frequently came to the throne. Their actual control over the person of the king resulted in these officials becoming the most powerful office holders in the entire kingdom. The royal court on occasion resided in important cities and yet also rested for weeks at a time in country palaces located around these cities. Public buildings from the Roman period served as the royal residences whether in the city or in the countryside. In the east, the most important royal cities were Rheims and Metz, in the west Paris, Soissons, and Rouen, and in Burgundy first Orléans and then Chalon-sur-Saône.

The regional administration of the larger kingdoms was based fundamentally on a late classical foundation, even if the former Roman provincial boundaries were no longer in use. The leading subdivision of these regions were the *civitates*, the cities with the area surrounding them. The chief officer here was the *comes*, a count, who was the permanent representative of the king in the area. He was responsible for the administration of justice, military affairs, as well as the civil administration. Following this model, the less urbanized areas of northern Gaul also received counts whose areas of jurisdiction were called *pagi*, that is districts. It was possible in all regions of the kingdom for a number of counts to be placed under the command of a *dux*, a duke. These dukes generally were assigned the highest military commands. East of the Rhine and in parts of southern Gaul and Burgundy, these ducal offices were made permanent and led to the creation of important centers of power. These duchies were especially important when they were used to organize local peoples such as the Alemanni, the Thuringians, and the Bavarians that had previously been independent.

In general, these *civitates* maintained their economic functions. On the one hand, they continued commercial production and on the other they provided a market for the foodstuffs required to sustain the cities. Agricultural production was not only determined by the *latifundia* of the Gallo-Roman aristocracy, who thanks to their numerous slaves were able to undertake the cultivation of specialized crops, but also by small farmers who were in part dependent on and in part independent from the great landowners. These structures were disrupted north of a line defined by Le Mans, Paris, and Meaux. In this region, small Roman farmers operated who were dependent on the royal courts as well as on ecclesiastical and lay magnates. The Franks themselves, for the most part, belonged to the ranks of the free small farmers. Very few of them were big landowners. They settled in small villages and used only the better lands, so that wide stretches of territory in eastern and northern Gaul remained uncultivated from the fifth century onwards. Specialized craft work was done only in a few places. In general, the farmers themselves produced what they needed in their daily lives. These conditions led to a strong decrease in the money economy.

The social structures of the Merovingian kingdom were exceptionally heterogeneous. There is evidence in the *Lex Salica* that old Francia, the core area of the Frankish lands, held a large class of farmers described as *ingenui*, the free. They had the right to bear arms and to represent themselves in legal matters. They settled their local problems within the context of a group of neighboring village settlements. Their blood price, that is the price that had to be paid to the relatives of a freeman who had been killed, was 200 shillings. The *laeti* or half-free, who were dependent on the free, participated in public life in only a limited manner. As was true of the Romans, they were protected by a blood price of 100 shillings. One should not underestimate the number of slaves who, according to early medieval legal concepts, stood nearer to animals and things than they did to people.

There is no mention of a Frankish nobility in the *Lex Salica*. Nevertheless, the Franks were familiar with an aristocracy whose members possessed a privileged position from birth. The members of this class, like the kings, were able to maintain a

military following utilizing their large landed and human resources. As a consequence, they were able to claim substantial
political importance. South of the Loire, the old Gallo-Roman
aristocracy, the senators, were able to maintain their superior
social and economic status at least into the seventh century. The
centers of noble life were the various royal courts of the contemporary Merovingian kings. The fathers were assigned to carry
out the various functions and offices of government while the
sons were brought up and prepared for their later roles. But royal
service also offered many simple freemen and even some unfree
the opportunity for very fast social promotion. At the same
time, unreliability or even lack of loyalty could lead to the undo-
ing of many noble office holders and to the social decline of
their families.

Aside from the far north and some areas in the east, the Gallic
church had survived the fall of the *Imperium Romanum* and the
rise of the Frankish kingdom largely unscathed. As was true of
the empire generally, the church was organized according to late
classical administrative principles. A *civitas*, understood as a
city with its surrounding territory, was usually identical with
the bishopric and was ruled by the bishop in monarchical style.
Similarly, the church province was identical with the Roman
province and was led by a metropolitan. This latter churchman
participated in the elevation of bishops and led the provincial
synods. In the sixth century, Gaul had eleven church provinces
and 128 bishoprics. The importance of the metropolitans declined over the course of the sixth century as the influence of the
kings in church politics grew. The bishops supervised all of the
churches, ecclesiastical institutions, church property, and charit-
able works. In addition, from the late classical period onward,
they played an increasing role in the secular administration of

their *civitas*. This was due, in part, to the fact that many of the bishops were recruited from the senatorial aristocracy. In the south of Gaul, especially, the bishops undertook so many secular tasks that one can speak about "episcopal government." As a consequence, the kings chose the candidates for bishoprics from among their trusted supporters and gave very little heed to the canonical forms which required election by the clergy and people. They continued to employ the senatorial, i.e. Gallo-Roman, nobility. However, over the course of time, the Frankish aristocracy also began to have an interest in ecclesiastical careers. The ties between the church and the Merovingians are demonstrated most clearly by the large number of Frankish synods. The first of these was held at Orléans in 511 as noted above. The synods dealt with questions of law, administration, and the regulation of the cult. However, their orientation toward Rome did not go beyond a veneration of Saint Peter.

Genealogical coincidences led to a brief period of reunification of the entire Frankish kingdom under Clothar I, the son of Clovis. When Clothar died in 561, he left, like his father, four sons. The kingdom was again divided among the four sons. And, again, one of the sons died shortly thereafter leading to the redistribution of the kingdom into three parts. This division formed the basis for the later sub-kingdoms of Austrasia (in the east) with its capital at Rheims, Neustria (in the west) with its capital at Paris, and Burgundy with its capital at Orléans. The bloody battles among Clothar's sons and their successors pushed the Frankish kingdom into an almost continuous series of civil wars up to 613. The rival kings were dependent on their nobles for support and these latter must therefore be understood as the true victors of the period of civil war. Because the individual groups of nobles became increasingly concentrated in one or another of the sub-kingdoms, the stabilization of the latter was a further important consequence of the struggles among the Merovingian kings.

In 613, Clothar II, a grandson of Clothar I, took control over a unified Frankish kingdom after defeating his cousins. The rise to power of both of the crucial figures in Carolingian family history is tied to his name. Arnulf, who had called the king to Austrasia in 613, became bishop of the Austrasian capital city of Metz. In this early period, Pippin I, who had worked closely with Arnulf, remained in the background. Lothar ruled from Paris which became, as it had been for a period during the reign of Clothar I, the capital of the entire Frankish kingdom. The king could not and did not wish to alter the independent status of the sub-kingdoms. Thus Clothar made an accommodation with the Austrasian nobility when, in 623, he established his eldest son Dagobert as king there. The new king's advisors were Bishop Arnulf of Metz and Pippin I, who was now the mayor of the palace. After Clothar's death in 629/30, Dagobert became the ruler of the entire Frankish kingdom and, like his father, resided most of the time at Paris. Dagobert also came to an accommodation with the Austrasian nobility when in 633/34 he established his two-year-old son Sigibert III as (sub) king in the eastern sub-kingdom.

Dagobert's death in 639 marks the beginning of the decline of the Merovingian dynasty as his generally underage or immature successors were unable to have any influence on the contemporary political situation. In place of these *rois fainéants*, do-nothing kings, the noble groups now took control of the kingdom. Their leading representatives strove to gain the office of mayor of the palace. This guaranteed control over the dependent kings who remained the indispensable carriers of legitimacy.

The violent struggles within the Frankish kingdom deepened the split between Neustria and Austrasia. The weakened Franks were no longer able to maintain their control over Aquitaine or the right bank of the Rhine. These areas developed into virtually independent duchies.

Following Dagobert's death, he was succeeded by his underage sons Sigibert III in Austrasia and Clovis II in Neustria–Burgundy. Following a struggle for power with his rival nobles, Pippin's son Grimoald became mayor of the palace in Austrasia. Sigibert died in 656/57. At this point, Grimoald had Sigibert's young son Dagobert sent into exile in Ireland and raised Childebert "the adopted" to the throne. Childebert may have been Grimoald's son who had been adopted by Sigibert. However, it is also possible that he was the true second son of Sigibert whom Grimoald used to further strengthen his position in Austrasia. New intra-Austrasian fighting broke out at this point. Finally, the Neustrians, under the leadership of their queen Balthild, the widow of Clovis II, and their mayor of the palace, Ebroin, entered the fray and removed Grimoald. King Childebert was replaced in 662/63 by Balthild's son called Childebert II. However, by 675, Grimoald's nephew and heir Pippin II was able to gain power again in Austrasia.

Pippin's moment came when conflict within the Neustrian nobility opened the way west to him. In 687, he defeated Berchar, the Neustrian mayor of the palace in battle at Tertry on the Somme. The murder of his rivals the next year made Pippin the *de facto* ruler in the Frankish kingdom. Pippin himself returned to Austrasia leaving behind King Theoderic III, who, although he resided in Neustria, was now king of the entire Frankish kingdom. Theoderic was watched over by Pippin's loyal followers there. However, the struggles among the Frankish nobles in the

The Carolingian Dynasty

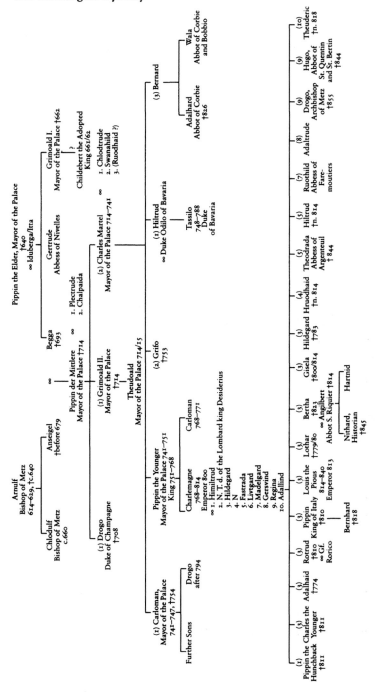

core of Frankish territory permitted the dukes of the adjacent regions, namely Aquitaine, Alemannia, Bavaria, and Thuringia, to consolidate their *de facto* independent status. It was only in Alemannia that Pippin was able to take advantage of a struggle among the heirs of Duke Gottfried to gain influence there through a number of military interventions in the period 709–712.

Pippin's success was due in large part to his marriage to Plectrude who came from one of the powerful Austrasian noble clans. From early on, Pippin gave important responsibilities to Plectrude's sons Drogo and Grimoald in Burgundy and Neustria, thereby marking them as his political heirs. Charles, whose mother Chalpaida also came from an influential family, had to accept a subordinate position behind his half-brothers for the time being. However, Drogo died in 708, and Grimoald was murdered in 714. The subsequent arrangements for Pippin's succession were largely determined by Plectrude who was to act as regent and rule in place of her grandchildren.

Nonetheless when Pippin died in 714, a number of noble factions turned against Plectrude's government. The decisive moment came when her grandson Theudoald was defeated in battle at Compiègne in 715 by the Neustrians, who were then able to seize control over the person of the Merovingian king. As had been the case earlier, the main battle line was between the Austrians and the Neustrians. In 716, under the leadership of their mayor of the palace Raganfred, the Neustrians were able to penetrate up to the Maas and even as far as Cologne. At this point, many Austrasians abandoned Pippin II's widow and turned to his son Charles, who from the ninth century was given the epithet *martellus*, the hammer, because of his military energy. In 717/18, Charles defeated the Neustrians and took possession of the Merovingian king whom he used as a puppet to legitimize his own rule.

Charles Martel ruled the Frankish kingdom with an iron hand and crushed his opponents. He conquered numerous *civitates* in Burgundy which had become almost independent under the leadership of their local bishops. Parts of church lands fell into his hands. He was heavily criticized for this in church circles long after his death during the ninth century when the political background for his policies had partly been forgotten. In fact, he maintained a very clever ecclesiastical policy and maneuvered skillfully among the various factions within the Frankish church. Although he supported the reformers such as those found in the circles around Willibrord and Boniface, he did not break off his relationship with the established and partly secular bishops such as Milo of Trier. It was this same Milo who was heavily condemned by Boniface who, after 719, served as a missionary bishop under Charles' protection.

Charles, however, was not content with his successes within the kingdom and sought to enforce central control over the peripheral regions of the Frankish realm. He was able to eliminate the local rulers of Thuringia, Alsace, and Alemannia, and to conquer Frisia. He was able to use conflicts with the ducal family of Bavaria to expand his influence there too. In 725, he took the Bavarian princess Swanahild back to the Frankish Kingdom and, now a widower, married her. In 736, Charles was to impose Odilo, a close relative of Swanahild, as his dependent duke in Bavaria. In order to consolidate his position in Bavaria and Alemannia, Charles maintained good relations with the Lombard king Liutprand (712–744). This relationship also served Charles in his struggle against the Arabs.

After they had completed their conquest of the Visigothic

kingdom of Spain in 711, the Arabs launched increasingly frequent attacks over the Pyrenees and threatened Aquitaine. In 732, they defeated the Aquitanian duke Eudo, who up to that point had maintained a successful defense against them, and advanced further north. At the request of Eudo, Charles Martel moved against the invaders. He defeated them between Tours and Poitiers. Contemporaries celebrated this as a victory of the Christians over the pagans. Nevertheless, it would be an exaggeration to describe this event as the salvation of the West, even if Charles halted the advance of the Saracens, as the Muslims were called by westerners. Within just three years Charles was able to gain control of Aquitaine. He strengthened Frankish influence against both internal and Muslim forces in southern Burgundy and Provence. He refrained, however, from any attacks on Italy. Here, the pope in Rome was continually under threat from the Lombards who wished to bring the eternal city under their control. When Gregory III asked Charles for aid in 739/40 and offered him a protectorship over the city of Rome, Charles declined, preferring his close relationship with Liutprand. After all, the city of Rome was still part of the Byzantine empire and the least that Charles could expect from any intervention on his part would be to irritate the east Roman emperor.

In any event, the pope's offer demonstrates that Charles' successes had returned the Frankish kingdom to its earlier status. The status of the mayor of the palace was correspondingly strong within the kingdom. As a result of his successes, Charles Martel ruled the Frankish kingdom like a king during the latter years of his life. The Merovingian king Theoderic IV, whom Charles had enthroned, was completely under his control. Following Theoderic's death in 737, Charles declined to invest another king. In contrast to his predecessors, Charles did not require a shadow king to legitimize his position. Even without the royal title, he was the highest representative of the Frankish kingdom both internally and externally. Did Charles strive for the kingship for himself or at least for his sons? He sent his second son Pippin to the Lombard kingdom and had him adopted by King Liutprand. It is not recorded whether he did so in order that Pippin, now elevated to the status of a king's son, could take on higher responsibilities. Whatever the reason, it is clear that Charles firmly established his family at the pinnacle of the Frankish kingdom and succeeded in leading it through the crises of the second half of the seventh century and the first half of the eighth.

Admittedly, Charles' division of his inheritance led to new difficulties. He marked out as his heirs both his elder sons from his first marriage, Carloman and Pippin, and Grifo his son by Swanahild. The kingdom was to be divided among them. However, after Charles' death in October 741, both sides claimed more than had been assigned to them. Grifo and his mother Swanahild sought support from Odilo of Bavaria, who at this time was married to Charles' daughter from his first marriage, Hiltrud. Odilo's union with Charles had been brought about by the intervention of Swanahild. Carloman and Pippin reacted very quickly, defeating their half-brother and stepmother in the same year, and imprisoning both of them. In 742, they re-divided the kingdom among themselves. They both took parts of Austrasia and Neustria in an effort to eliminate the lingering hostility between these two regions. The brothers also maintained a unified front as the Alemanni, Bavarians, and Aquitanians had all risen in revolt against them. The situation had become so dangerous that in 743, Carloman and Pippin again raised up a Merovingian, Childerich III, as king in order to strengthen their own legitmacy. In the same year, they were able to defeat their most dangerous opponent, Odilo of Bavaria. By 745 they had finally defeated the last of their opponents.

In church affairs, Carloman and Pippin collaborated with Boniface, who was working toward a closer relationship between the Frankish church and Rome. With the agreement of the pope, he founded three new bishoprics during the 740s in the Thuringian-Hessian area of his mission: Erfurt, Würzburg, and Büraburg. During the same period Boniface called a number of Frankish synods with the support of Carloman and Pippin. One item on the agenda was the restoration of property taken from the churches and monasteries, that is compensation in the form of donations. Additional items included improving the control of bishops over their dioceses, and tying the church hierarchy more closely to Rome through the (re-)establishment of the archiepiscopal office. In the West, the archbishop took the place of the metropolitan as the head of a church province. The sign of his office was the *pallium*, which could only be bestowed by the pope. In this manner, closer ties were established between the various regional churches and Rome. Despite Boniface's intentions, however, he was the only archbishop appointed, and his successor Chrodegang of Metz saw his role more as an aid to Frankish central government than as a representative of the pope. Nevertheless, he and other powerful reformers successfully carried on Boniface's work after his death in 754.

Carloman and Pippin again worked together in a brotherly fashion toward church reform, although Carloman took the lead here and had a better relationship with Boniface. The situation that was intimated in this area soon became generally apparent: Carloman and Pippin began to pursue different interests. The estrangement between the two brothers reached its peak in 747

when Carloman abdicated. Carloman was religiously motivated, at least that was what was said later in Pippin's circle, to
give up his position and to establish his eldest son Drogo as his
heir and successor. Carloman left for Rome as a cleric and a
short time later became a monk at Monte Casino. Pippin's ambitions as well as his support among his followers grew after his
wife Bertrada, after four years of marriage, bore him a son on 2
April 748 named Charles after his grandfather. In the face of
Pippin's opposition, Carloman's son Drogo was no longer able
to maintain himself as a partner in power. Grifo, whom Pippin
had set free, turned against his half-brother, was conquered,
but maintained his legal claim to an equal share in government.
Drogo and his younger brother may have acted in the same
fashion.

The situation in the Frankish kingdom was therefore still
uncertain when Pippin sent his famous question to Pope Zacharias, "whether it was a good thing or not that kings in the Frankish kingdom had no royal power." The successor of Saint Peter
at this time required support against the Lombards and gave the
desired answer of no. Encouraged by this statement, Pippin had
himself made king at Soissons in 751. The Franks acclaimed and
paid homage to him. Then, following the model set forth in the
Old Testament, Pippin was anointed with holy oil in order to
legitimize his kingdom symbolically as coming "from God's
grace." The Merovingian Childerich was deposed, shorn as a
monk, and incarcerated in a monastery. Thus, the almost
century-long process by which the Carolingians replaced the
Merovingians came to an end. In Pippin, the Franks now had a
ruler who was king not only in name but in fact as well.

When the new pope Stephen II was again threatened by the
Lombard king Aistulf, Pippin invited him to his kingdom in 753.

Pippin used this opportunity to further increase the reputation of his still-young kingship through a meeting with the representative of Saint Peter. Stephen accepted the invitation and Pippin sent his eldest son Charles, then not even six years old, to meet the pope. On 6 January 754, Pippin received the pope personally at a festive assembly in the palace of Ponthion. Aistulf reacted by sending Carloman to the Frankish kingdom in order to oppose the threatened papal-Frankish alliance. Considerations of how his sons had been disinherited may also have motivated the former mayor of the palace to take this step. Despite the opposition of many Frankish magnates, however, Pippin was still able to gain general acceptance. Carloman was arrested and at almost the same time his sons were finally excluded from the possibility of succession and forcibly tonsured as monks. Carloman, who was already a monk, became sick a short time later and died in Vienne in 754 under the care of his sister-in-law Bertrada. It was probably in the same year that Grifo died in battle fighting against his brother's frontier troops. He had attempted to cross the Alps in order find refuge among the Lombards.

Thus, at almost one blow, Pippin was now freed from any competition from within his family. Nevertheless, he strove to secure his kingship and the rights of his descendants. At the end of July 754, he had himself, together with his sons Charlemagne and Carloman (born 751), anointed, this time personally by the pope. It is also possible that at this time Stephen II decided that the Franks were not to choose their kings from any other family. This was directed both against the Merovingians and against the distaff lines of the ruling Carolingian dynasty. In the same vein, he administered the sacrament of confirmation to Pippin's sons as well and formed in that way a spiritual relationship (*compaternitas*) with the new Frankish dynasty. Pippin gained even more prestige when the pope granted him the title of *patricius Romanorum*, protector of the Romans.

Pippin was fully deserving of this special responsibility toward the eternal city and Peter the leader of the apostles. Already in April, during an assembly at Quierzy, he had promised large parts of central Italy to the pope in a document known as the "Donation of Pippin." Of course, these lands first had to be taken from the Lombards. In order to accomplish this task, Pippin crossed the Alps late in the summer of 754. Despite the fact that internal Frankish opposition had limited the size of the army he could bring into the field, he defeated Aistulf and besieged him at his capital of Pavia. The Lombard king had to give up the territories that he had just conquered from the Byzantines, particularly Ravenna, and to recognize Frankish overlordship. In 756, Pippin was again forced to appear in Italy in order to force Aistulf to keep this peace agreement.

Aside from the establishment of Carolingian kingship and the development of closer relations with the papacy, Pippin's greatest achievement was his conquest of Aquitaine. Admittedly, Frankish control in this duchy had been growing since the days of Charles Martel, and this control had been further strengthened by Pippin and Carloman. Now, however, Pippin completed the conquest. From 760 on, Pippin launched almost annual campaigns against Aquitaine which finally brought the duchy to its knees. In 768, Waifar, the last duke, was murdered by his own supporters. Pippin, who benefited from and who may have instigated this act, very quickly thereafter added Aquitaine to the Frankish kingdom. However, the fifty-four-year-old Pippin did not have long to enjoy his success for he died on 24 September of the same year.

III

CHARLEMAGNE'S YOUTH AND THE FIRST YEARS OF HIS REIGN

From Son of the Mayor of the Palace to Conqueror of Italy

From a certain point of view, it can be a disadvantage if the contemporaries of an important person have concerned themselves with his *vita*. A good example of this phenomenon is Einhard's *Vita Karoli* which has long conditioned our knowledge of Charlemagne. Concerning Charlemagne's early years, Einhard wrote, "I consider it foolish to discuss his birth, childhood, or youth, because there is nothing in writing about this time, and there is no one still alive who could claim to have knowledge about these matters." On another occasion in his work, Einhard noted that Charlemagne died on 28 January 814 at the age of 72. Did he know the year of birth despite the alleged poor state of information concerning this early period? Yet his report of the date is incorrect as we know from sources that have survived up to the present day that Charlemagne was born on 2 April 748. Einhard's claims that there was no one left alive who knew something about Charlemagne's childhood are also incorrect. Indeed, there are sources, with which Einhard was undoubtedly familiar, which report that Charlemagne met with the pope at the end of 753. It is therefore necessary to consider Einhard's claims very carefully since they were probably influenced by motives other than an ardent desire for truth. He provides an accurate death date for Charlemagne because Einhard's literary model Suetonius—the Roman historian—had given such dates in his lives of the ancient caesars. He refrained from describing his hero's childhood and youth because to do so would have reminded his audience of the great struggles within the dynasty between Pippin, Grifo, and Carloman along with the latter's sons. They did not fit within the harmonious picture which Einhard wished to draw of Charlemagne and his father.

What then do we know about Charlemagne's birth, childhood, and youth? When he was born on 2 April 748, Charlemagne was the eldest son of his father Pippin. For a long time it was unforeseeable that he would rule as king over the Frankish empire. Charlemagne's father was the most powerful but not the only mayor of the palace. At this time, Pippin's nephew Drogo, Carloman's successor, was still entitled to be mayor of the palace. In addition, Drogo's brothers as well as his father's half brother Grifo also had legitimate claims to participation in ruling the kingdom. As noted earlier, Pippin was able to exclude all of these competitors from within his own family as well as the Merovingian king himself to become sole ruler and eventually king. These were the decisive conditions for Charlemagne's success even if he did have to share power for the time being with his brother Carloman who was born in 751.

Pippin certainly gave a great deal of thought when choosing the name "Charles" for his first born son, in remembrance of Charles Martel, the boy's grandfather. Pippin wished to signal that his son would follow in the footsteps of the great mayor of the palace and advertised this claim for him. This step was even more important because Pippin's brother Carloman had not established his elder son Drogo in this tradition. The reason for this was that Charles Martel was still alive when Drogo was born, and people generally avoided naming a child after a living relative. But what did this name "Charles," which was uncommon in this period, actually mean? For a while it was thought that the name was taken from the root in "Kerl = fellow/man" which meant "a free man without inherited property," or simply "man, married man, or beloved." This interpretation of "Charles" was used to support the now outdated theory that Charles Martel's mother Chalpaida came from a low-status family. Modern research sees the name "Carolus" as the Romanized form of "Hariolus" a pet form of the name "Chario." It also appears to have been an element in the name "Charibert" which was borne by two Merovingian kings. There is also some suggestion that the name may have been derived from "Crallo." This was the name of the father of Bishop Kunibert of Cologne, who had been a close ally of Pippin the Elder. In any case, there were no negative connotations associated with the name "Charles" at the end of the seventh century. Any remaining negative associations were certainly dispersed through the course of Charles Martel's successful reign. It is therefore not surprising that following this tradition Pippin also named his second son Carloman.

It is true that we have very few details concerning the early life of Charlemagne, even if the record is not as sparse as his biographer Einhard would have us believe. He appeared for the first time in public at the meeting with Pope Stephen II held at the end of 753. In July 754, Charlemagne along with his father and his three-year-old brother Carloman were anointed as kings by the pope. However, neither he nor Carloman assumed the royal title before the death of their father. Almost exactly one year later on 25 July 755, the king and his two sons took part in the transfer of the relics of Saint Germanus. The event made such a deep impression on young Charlemagne that he still told of it during his later years.

At least the first two events mentioned here took place during Charlemagne's childhood (*infantia*) which, according to contemporary views, lasted until the seventh year. Generally, children of the nobility spent their first years under the care of their mothers. But they were also looked after by their wet nurses and later by their teachers. Their "training" began at about six years of age. The sons of the nobility learned to ride, to use weapons, and to hunt. An author from the ninth century wrote that "children and youths in the households of the magnates are raised to endure hardship and adversity such as hunger, cold, and heat. A well known popular proverb says: whoever is not well trained in mounted warfare by the time he reaches puberty, will only be able to acquire this skill with great difficulty, if at all, at a later age." Charlemagne is supposed to have been raised "in all the prudence of the world," as we learn from the *vita* of his cousin Adalhard. Here, we are dealing less with school learning than with the knowledge of how to behave in noble society, especially at court and in the king's council. The phase of *pueritia* or boyhood, lasted up to about the fifteenth year. Then followed the *adolescentia*, youth which lasted from the age of 14 to 28. These are not too dissimilar to contemporary notions of youth.

In the early Middle Ages one came of age at the end of *pueritia*. According to the *Lex Salica*, one was legally capable at the age of 12. The *Lex Ribuaria* gave 15 as the age of legal responsibility. These numbers indicate how "young" secular society was. As long as they lived in their fathers' households, even sons who were of age were under the guardianship of their fathers. It was only when they had established their own households that they obtained full freedom of action, at least theoretically. Frequently, a son's marriage caused such a change in status. All the same a king had to give thought in advance about how to prepare his sons for their future duties. Pippin did this by having first Charlemagne and then his brother Carloman take an increasing public role after 760. Thus, for example, in 760 he placed the monastery of Saint-Calais near Le Mans under his own protection as well as the protection of Charlemagne. The next year Pippin took Charlemagne with him on campaign in Aquitaine. In 762, Pippin took Carloman along as well. Again in 762, both sons confirmed a charter made by their parents to the monastery of Prüm. They were thus given personal experience in the practice of the royal office.

A short time later, Pippin allowed his sons to act more independently. During an assembly at Worms in 763, Pippin assigned to them the administration of several counties. Unfortunately, it is not said where these counties were located. It is likely, however, that Charlemagne was given control of the region around Le Mans where he already had responsibility for the monastery of Saint-Calais. This region lay on the edge of the territories actually controlled by the king. The influential nobles living there tended to stand in opposition to the king. Indeed, Charlemagne's uncle Grifo had already found support here. This task doubtlessly put the fifteen-year-old's abilities to the test. The city of Worms saw the full entry of the two royal sons into the adult world. On this occasion, a father usually gave his son a sword. This ceremony was a symbolic demonstration that the son's training as a warrior had come to an end. Even Pope Paul I sent gifts to the brothers. These, however, were lost in transit. In a letter sent at the beginning of the following year, the pope addressed the two royal sons almost as co-rulers with their father.

It was only shortly before his death that Pippin arranged the succession in detail. In early autumn of 768, he returned to Saint-Denis from his final campaign in Aquitaine. The fifty-four-year-old king was very ill and felt that his end was near. Numerous ecclesiastical and secular magnates gathered around the dying man and approved his final decisions concerning his inheritance. He divided the kingdom geographically as it had been divided between him and his brother Carloman in 742. The old realms of Neustria and Austrasia were once again divided. Pippin did the same with newly conquered Aquitaine. Charlemagne received the western and northern parts of these three regions. His kingdom stretched from the south-west Pyrenees to the far bank of the Rhine and ran in a half circle around his brother's realm.

Pippin died on 24 September 768 and like his father Charles Martel was buried at Saint-Denis, which was the most important burial site for the Merovingian dynasty he had overthrown. Two weeks later, on 9 October, which was the feast day of Denis, the patron saint of the Frankish rulers, Pippin's sons were raised to the kingship. This occurred in the neighboring cities of Noyon (Charlemagne) and Soissons (Carloman). This coordinated series of events indicates that plans had already been made while Pippin was still alive. However, within a year, the brothers disregarded their father's arrangements. It is said that after drawing lots, all of Aquitaine fell to Charlemagne, a fact that would soon lead to conflict with his brother. There might have been a further cause of contention between the two brothers arising from Charlemagne's private possession of the monastery of Saint-Dié in the middle of Carloman's territory. In January 769, Charlemagne granted this monastery to Saint-Denis thereby securing a burial place for himself in the old royal vault which lay in Carloman's sub-kingdom. Perhaps Charlemagne felt that he had been slighted somewhat in his father's division of the kingdom, because his younger brother had been granted the royal vault at Saint-Denis and the old royal city of Soissons. In addition, Charlemagne had no territorial access to Italy and was thereby cut off from Rome and the Pope.

Aquitaine turned out to be a somewhat problematic inheritance as Hunald, the son of Waifar, rebelled against the Frankish occupiers. Charlemagne reacted quickly to this revolt and marched into Aquitaine in early 769. He appealed in vain to his brother for support. Even a personal meeting at Duasdives (in the neighborhood of Vienne) brought no success. Nevertheless, Charlemagne was victorious in the campaign. It is unknown why Carloman refused to help his brother. Had Charlemagne infringed on his father's settlement by bringing all of Aquitaine illegally under his control? Had Carloman demanded a price for his aid that Charlemagne was unwilling to pay? Or perhaps, was the relationship between the two brothers so strained by earlier events that there could be no question of Carloman giving aid to Charlemagne? Whatever the circumstances, shortly thereafter the two brothers had a brief reconciliation which even caused Pope Stephen III himself to express joy in far-off Rome. The pope hoped that Charlemagne and Carloman would support him against the Lombard king Desiderius. This hope was in vain, however, as new tensions between the Frankish kings excluded any possibility of joint action.

The rivalry between the two brothers also became manifest in another area. Both brothers married early and named their first sons Pippin after their father. In this manner, the brothers recalled the great model of their father and his successful predecessors and thereby presented themselves to their supporters as guarantors of the continuation of this tradition into the next generation. Charlemagne had an initial advantage in this competition to continue the dynasty. His wife Himiltrud bore a son in 769/70 so that their son was the elder of the two "Pippin" grandsons. Because of a deformity, which may only have appeared later on, this child received the epithet "the hunchback." In 770, Carloman's wife Gerberga also had a son who was completely healthy. The fact that Carloman chose the name "Pippin," which had already been used, must be understood as a serious provocation. By choosing this name, Carloman set himself in direct competition with his brother. The future would show which of the two Pippins was able to rule. Carloman had another son whose name and year of birth are not known. However, the true conflict between the brothers hung on the question of which one would be able to claim the leading position in the Carolingian dynasty.

The escalating conflict between Charlemagne and Carloman brought Bertrada, the widow of Pippin and the mother of Charlemagne and Carloman, onto the scene. For a woman of that period, even for a queen, she was unusually active in her efforts to end the conflict between her sons, apparently favoring Charlemagne. In May 770 she met with Carloman in Selz (Alsace) for the sake of peace (*pacis causa*). The meeting, however, brought no success. Then, the queen planned that Charlemagne should marry a daughter of the Lombard king Desiderius. His relationship with Himiltrud did not pose a problem in this context because up to this point the church had not been able to enforce the indissolubility of marriage. This marriage was to lead to a political alliance that would isolate Carloman. His realm could be threatened by Charlemagne and Desiderius from the north, west, and south. This left only the east. It is therefore telling that in order to realize her plan Bertrada first traveled to Bavaria and conferred with Duke Tassilo III. Tassilo was a cousin of Charlemagne and Carloman and had, in addition, married another daughter of the Lombard king named Liutbirg. If he joined the alliance against Carloman, then the encirclement would be complete.

The approach by Bertrada and Charlemagne to the Lombards marked a break with Pippin's Italian policies as the latter had always protected the papacy from the Lombards. Pope Stephen III reacted very indignantly. Since he did not yet know which of the two Frankish kings was to marry the Lombard, he wrote to both of them and cautioned against an alliance "with the faithless and most vile Lombard people which do not count among the ranks of the peoples and whose members have certainly brought forth the lepers." This coarse language can be explained by the heavy pressure that the Lombards were again bringing to bear against Rome at the time. The marriage project would have increased this pressure and the pope therefore saw it as a break in the alliance that had been established between Pippin and his sons and the successor of the prince of the apostles. Carloman reacted immediately since he saw the opportunity to win, or rather to keep an ally. He sent a high-level embassy to Rome and asked the pope to stand as godfather to his newly born second son. The spiritual tie with the pope was intended to counterbalance Charlemagne's real relationship with the Lombard king.

Certainly Charlemagne, and especially Bertrada, did not wish this alliance between Carloman and the pope to come into being. While Bertrada negotiated with Desiderius in Pavia, she convinced him to make significant concessions to the pope. After this, Bertrada went to Rome and was able to convince the pope to approve of the alliance between Charlemagne and Desiderius, including the marriage project. The pope refrained from becoming godfather to Carloman's son. The letters that Stephen wrote to Charlemagne and Bertrada in the following period are evidence that they had a good relationship. Desiderius largely kept the promises that he had made at Pavia. It is possible that during her return from Rome, Bertrada again stopped at the Lombard capital and brought along Charlemagne's bride-to-be. However, the name of this girl has not come down to us. Desiderius' desire that his son Adelchis be married to Charlemagne's thirteen-year-old sister Gisela did not come to pass. This did not, however, disrupt the overall plan. Carloman now stood alone against his brother and his neighbors in the south and east.

Carloman sought to re-establish some room for political maneuvering by intervening at Rome. He sent one of his trusted men to Rome in order to convince the pope to change his mind using any possible means. This man won the support of influential circles at the papal court, and Desiderius was so disturbed by this turn of events that he appeared at Rome with an army during Lent of 771 and disrupted these efforts. In reaction, Carloman is reported to have planned an attack on Rome and Pope Stephen. With the situation so strained in Rome and Italy, the Frankish kingdom could not remain unaffected. Neither Charlemagne nor Carloman undertook any military actions against external foes, and both of them remained on their borders during the autumn of 771. It must remain a point of speculation whether they were planning to go to war against each other.

However, in his biography of Charlemagne, Einhard does tell of warmongers. Of course, according to Einhard, these men only appeared in Carloman's court. In any case, matters took a different turn.

On 4 December 771, Carloman died at the young age of 20 at the palace of Samoussy near Laon. Charlemagne was the only beneficiary of Carloman's death and at one stroke became the sole ruler of the Frankish kingdom. This sudden death brought about an entirely new state of affairs. Charlemagne reacted immediately to news of Carloman's death. He hurried to the neighborhood of Laon and summoned to Corbeny his dead brother's magnates under the leadership of Archbishop Wilchar of Sens, the highest ecclesiastical official in the Frankish kingdom, and Abbot Fulrad of Saint-Denis, who had headed the court chapel under Pippin and Carloman. They paid homage to Charlemagne who thereby reestablished the unity of the Frankish kingdom despite the fact that his brother had left behind two sons. Carloman's widow Gerberga did not put up a struggle. After her husband had been buried at Rheims, she fled with her children and a few supporters to the only king in the region who could offer her protection, that is to King Desiderius, Charlemagne's father-in-law. A struggle would have been pointless. Offered the choice between a 23-year-old king and a small child, the magnates in the kingdom would have decided to support the experienced candidate. As had happened frequently in Frankish history, an adult uncle was able to prevail against his underage nephew.

Following Carloman's death there was a complete reversal of alliances. Desiderius took in Gerberga and her children. Although he had been an opponent of Carloman, he had an interest in the continued division of the Frankish kingdom, a situation which was much more favorable to him than the concentration of power in the hands of a single ruler. Desiderius was also the only one who could help Gerberga and her children to achieve their rights. At this time he was the father-in-law of both Charlemagne and Tassilo of Bavaria, and therefore the most powerful king in western Europe. In addition, he also controlled the city of Rome and indirectly the papacy as well. Charlemagne viewed the granting of asylum to Gerberga and her children at the Lombard court as a hostile act and therefore cast out Desiderius' daughter after just one year of marriage, which had the nearly the same meaning as a declaration of war against the Lombard king.

Despite these provocations, the two rulers surprisingly took no action against each other in 772. Rather, each tried to strengthen his own position. Desiderius induced Hadrian, who was elected pope in February 772, to continue the pro-Lombard policies of his predecessor Stephen and demanded that he consecrate Carloman's sons as kings of the Franks. In this manner, Desiderius would not only have helped the boys to achieve exceptional prestige, which would have transformed them into true competitors to Charlemagne; he would also have hindered the renewal of the alliance between the papacy and a unified Frankish realm for the foreseeable future. The reaction in the Frankish kingdom to the dismissal of his daughter shows that Desiderius' political actions were not completely hopeless. For his part, Charlemagne sought to find a new wife whose family was sufficiently politically powerful to replace what he had lost by ending his marriage with Desiderius' daughter. Charlemagne's third wife Hildegard was descended on her mother's side from the old Alemmanic ducal house and was also a cousin of the Bavarian duke Tassilo. As Desiderius' son-in-law, Tassilo is unlikely to have approved of the dismissal of his sister-in-law by Charlemagne. By establishing another family tie between them, Charlemagne was able at least to induce the powerful Bavarian duke to remain neutral in the coming struggle.

The same year, Charlemagne became militarily active and launched an attack on the Saxons, which at first glance does not appear to be connected to recent events. Among other actions, Charlemagne destroyed the Irminsul, a central shrine for the pagan Saxons. One might think that Charlemagne had dissipated his strength and opened a new front before his disrupted relationship with Desiderius was settled one way or another. However, Charlemagne's first campaign against the Saxons also brought considerable advantages in his conflict against Desiderius. Following his victory over the rebellious Aquitanians, with his campaign against the Saxons Charlemagne provided his nobles with the opportunity for renewed successful military activity, and this strengthened his position as king. He captured the offerings, particularly gold and silver, that had been kept at the Irminsul, and had these transported to the Frankish kingdom. In so doing, Charlemagne not only got rich spoils, he significantly increased the value of the royal treasury as an important instrument of rulership. He was now in a position to reward the loyalty that his followers had shown in him during the conflict with Carloman. He could not have used the lands from his brother's territories for this because of the resident nobles. However, Charlemagne's supporters still awaited some reward in return for their loyalty. Charlemagne could well use the Saxon treasure to make good these "debts."

At that point, Charlemagne must have been very interested in acquiring the support of as many of the nobles as he could. He was very much dependent on the loyalty of his followers at this time as criticism had been voiced at his change of policy toward the Lombard king. Even his mother Bertrada did not support his decision since it was she, after all, who had negotiated the alliance with Desiderius. Charlemagne's cousin Adalhard retired from court in anger over this policy and joined the monastery of Corbie. It should not be underestimated that several of Carloman's leading supporters accompanied Gerberga and her sons into exile even if Charlemagne's historians indicate that there were only a few of them. They could nevertheless have become the seed of an effective opposition. However, Charlemagne's victory over the Saxons increased his prestige as king. Furthermore, the Saxon booty provided him with sufficient means to overcome the threats sketched here and to secure the loyalty of his supporters for the future.

Already at the beginning of 773, a request for help from Pope Hadrian reached Charlemagne. In the intervening period, the pope had weakened the pro-Lombard party in Rome of power and decided to refuse to consecrate Carloman's sons as kings. As a result, he was pressed harder and harder by Desiderius, who for a time had even occupied parts of Rome's territory. Hadrian supposedly had threatened excommunication to keep Desiderius from attacking Rome itself. Desiderius considered himself to be in an unassailable position of power and he refused several attempts at negotiation by Charlemagne. Charlemagne's willingness to oblige may be an indication that, like his father Pippin, he had taken into consideration a pro-Lombard party among his own supporters. They may have only put aside their reservations about a military intervention in the face of Desiderius' unwillingness to compromise.

The Franks did not cross the Alps before the late summer of 773. Charlemagne assembled his army near Geneva and divided it into two sections. He led the first over Mount Cenis into Italy. His uncle Bernard led the second force over the Great Saint Bernard Pass. Desiderius faced them at the Lombard narrows, the strong border fortifications located in the area around Susa. Charlemagne again attempted a diplomatic approach which was once more rejected by Desiderius. A Frankish encircling maneuver forced him to retreat. The Lombard king entrusted himself to the strong walls of his capital Pavia where Charlemagne besieged him. When Adelchis, Desiderius' son, along with Carloman's family, took up a fortified position at Verona, the Frankish ruler left his main army at Pavia and marched with a small force to Verona. Despite the fact that according to a contemporary Verona was supposed to have been one of the best fortified cities in the Lombard kingdom, Gerberga and her supporters are reported to have given themselves up voluntarily. However, since it appears that there was no fighting involved and that the Lombards still controlled Verona, it is probably the case that Adelchis handed Carloman's family over in order to get Charlemagne to retreat. The sources are silent about what then happened to Charlemagne's sister-in-law and his nephews.

Although the Franks captured several other cities in northern Italy, the war was finally decided at Pavia where Charlemagne returned from Verona. It was an almost impossible task to capture a well-fortified city such as Pavia, even for Frankish troops who, under Charlemagne's father Pippin, had used their superior siege techniques to conquer Aquitaine. The siege of Pavia began in September and had to be carried on through the fall and winter. It was trying for both the defenders and the attackers. After the siege had already lasted half a year, Charlemagne went to Rome for Easter in 774 with a substantial part of his army. There, Hadrian received him with the ceremonial honor granted to the exarch of Ravenna, the former chief official of the Byzantine emperor in Italy, and thereby stressed Charlemagne's role as the protector of Rome (*patricius Romanorum*). The festive Easter celebration at the tombs of the apostles may have lifted the spirits of the Frankish warriors and increased their motivation to carry out new deeds.

However, Charlemagne's first visit to Rome also had a political goal. The pope and the Frankish king strengthened the alliance established by their predecessors and in 774 Charlemagne renewed the "Donation of Pippin," thereby guaranteeing the papal possessions in central Italy. It is an open question whether he did this to counter a future possible threat by the Lombards to the pope as Charlemagne's ally or whether he had already decided, entirely for his own reasons, to eliminate the Lombard kingdom. Desiderius' determined resistance at Pavia may have convinced Charlemagne that a long-term solution in Italy could only be brought about once and for all by military means. In any event, Charlemagne returned to Pavia in April and reinforced his siege of the city, which was finally taken because of hunger and disease. At the beginning of June, after an almost nine-month-long siege, Desiderius surrendered. Desiderius was banished to a Frankish monastery. His son Adelchis was able to escape to the Byzantine empire.

Charlemagne thus opened up possibilities for himself that he could not have foreseen when the war began. He seized the Lombard treasury and took the Lombard kingship without a formal act of election. No later than 5 July 774, Charlemagne bore the title *rex Francorum et Langobardorum*, that is king of the Franks and Lombards. Charlemagne had ended the independence of the last great non-Frankish kingdom in continental Europe. Upper as well as central Italy now fell to the Frankish kingdom.

The independent Lombard principality of Benevento remained in the southern part the peninsula. It was still necessary to put down several revolts in the rest of Italy. Numerous Lombard nobles went into exile north of the Alps. In their place, Frankish, Alemmanic, Burgundian, and later Bavarian officials came into Italy and administered the former Lombard kingdom in the name of its new rulers.

Why did the Lombard kingdom collapse so quickly? How are we to explain Charlemagne's relatively effortless success which made him ruler of upper and central Italy? Certainly, Frankish military superiority was a factor, which was strengthened by Charlemagne's ability both to achieve quick tactical victories and to complete successfully prolonged operations. On the other hand, the Lombard kingdom clearly was much weaker than it had appeared to be. The inner unity of the Lombard nobles had diminished over time. Following the death of Liutprand in 744 many of the Lombard dukes had pursued their own policies and had secretly or even openly opposed the central government. The successes achieved by Aistulf and Desiderius against the Byzantines, Rome, and the pope covered over these inner weaknesses. Even before the Frankish invasion, many Lombard nobles already favored Charlemagne. When Desiderius failed to stop the Frankish advance at the narrows, numerous Lombards went over to the pope. Indeed, at Spoleto Hadrian was able to appoint a duke of his choice. The causes for the quick collapse of the Lombard kingdom were, therefore, Charlemagne's unquestionable skills as a politician and general, as well as the internal weakness of the state.

With the conquest of the Lombard kingdom Charlemagne effectively ended his "apprenticeship." He was transformed from a king's son and then a comparatively insecure young king whose mother still had him, so to speak, on a leash, into a victor over the Aquitanians, Saxons, Lombards, and into the conqueror of Italy. His determined and vigorous manner had proven to be a decisive advantage in his conflicts with external foes. He did not hesitate after the death of his brother. In his conflicts with the Lombards he demonstrated a quality that is even more important for a ruler, that is the stamina that helped him to see a nine-month siege to a successful end.

IV

THE EXPANSION OF THE FRANKISH KINGDOM IN THE EAST

Saxons, Bavarians, and Avars

In 772, Charlemagne launched his first campaign against the Saxons setting out from the middle Rhineland. According to Einhard, Charlemagne intended this campaign as a punishment of the Saxons for their constant attacks. However, as noted above, internal political considerations and preparations for war in Italy also played important roles. Charlemagne advanced to the upper Weser and claimed twelve hostages from the defeated Saxons. But did this mark the subjugation of the entire Saxon people or only some segments of the Saxon population? This question can hardly be answered because it was one of the peculiarities of the Saxons that they did not have one king. They were divided into numerous peoples and groups each of which had its own leader. These leaders were not described as "kings" by contemporary writers from the Frankish kingdom and the British isles. Nevertheless, in point of fact they can be thought of in this manner. Clearly, they could not be compared with the Frankish king or the Anglo-Saxon rulers. However, they were the highest representatives of their peoples and they may even have been venerated as cult figures as well. A unifying bond among the Saxons was the yearly meeting at Marklo on the Weser, which was attended by the kings and their retainers. A further institutional element binding together the Saxon tribes was the high command that was granted to one of their leaders in time of war. But during Charlemagne's long war against them, the Saxons latter do not appear to have had a military leadership. Their heterogeneity was to be the Saxons' greatest strength in their defensive battle against the Franks.

As Charlemagne conquered the Lombard kingdom in Italy in 773/74, the Saxons took their revenge for the Frankish attack of 772 by ravaging numerous Christian churches in northern Hesse, including the monastery of Fritzlar and the temporary episcopal seat at Büraburg. In the fall of 774 Charlemagne returned from Italy and sent four military detachments against the Saxons. At the royal assembly at Quierzy in January 775, he decided to follow a new strategy, namely, "to overwhelm in war the infidel and faithless Saxon people and to continue until they either had been defeated and subjugated to Christianity, or were completely annihilated." This was the account provided by a Frankish court annalist after Charlemagne's death, and was an accurate description of the contemporary situation. Because the Saxons had destroyed Christian churches, Charlemagne was challenged in his most important obligation as a ruler, namely as the protector of Christianity. Now at the latest a skirmish on the border became a conflict involving matters of faith. The Saxons clung to their old religion and worshipped gods such as Saxnot and Wodan. The Irminsul apparently played an important role in their religion. According to one later historian, it was a cult site in the form of a wooden column that was venerated for supposedly being a pillar of the universe.

It was probably the destruction of the Irminsul in 772 that led a large group of Saxons to invade the Frankish kingdom and to destroy Christian churches in an act of revenge. Charlemagne wanted revenge in turn, and in this manner the escalation of violence took its course. Did the king, accustomed to success, know what he had let himself in for? Was his policy directed against all of the Saxon groups or only against those who had first surrendered to him and then waged war on his kingdom? Were these two groups identical, or had only part of the Saxon people taken revenge for the destruction of the Irminsul without caring that other Saxons had subjected themselves to the Frankish king? Because of the fragmentation among the Saxons, these questions can only be answered with great difficulty. Charlemagne and the Franks do not appear to have had a great interest in differentiating among them and did not care about the state of affairs among the Saxons. Rather, they chose all the territories in the southern Saxon lands, those that bordered on the Frankish kingdom, as their operational goal. On the other hand, Saxons in the immediate vicinity of the powerful Frankish kingdom undoubtedly felt threatened. In defending themselves, all of them stood together so that the attacking Franks discerned three major groups among them: the Westphalians in the West, the Enger in the Weser region, and the Eastphalians in the East.

The implementation of the decision taken at Quierzy followed swiftly: Charlemagne marched in early 775 from the Lower Rhineland over the Eresburg toward the Weser. After he had successfully forced the crossing of this river, Charlemagne proceeded toward the Oker. Here, the Eastphalians appeared before the king under the leadership of a man named Hessi.

They gave hostages and swore oaths of loyalty. On the return march, the Enger, led by Brun, subjected themselves to Charlemagne. In the meantime, the Westphalians under the leadership of Widukind had faced and defeated a Frankish force that was supposed to secure the crossing over the Weser river. Charlemagne made up for this defeat with a victory near Lübbeke where he forced the Westphalians to submit and to hand over hostages. There is substantial evidence to suggest that Charlemagne annexed the territory from the Rhine along the Lippe up to the Eresburg at this time. As a result of this campaign, the Franks gained control over the Hellweg and with it an important connecting road to Hesse and Thuringia which made the slow detours through mountainous territory unnecessary. This campaign was thus a great success. But Charlemagne led the campaign with such brutality that in Northumbria in England it was recorded that he had raged with fire and sword to an extent that his sanity was doubted. There is no mention of missionary activity in any of the sources. In other words, according to the plan worked out at Quierzy, the Saxons were to be subjected to Frankish rule by any means necessary. Their Christianization played only a minor role, if any, in these plans.

In 776, Charlemagne was forced to hurry to Italy in order to put down a revolt by Lombard turncoats. His Saxon enemies took this opportunity to rise up and strike at the Frankish conquests in southern Saxony. Charlemagne succeeded, in the same year, in marching to Italy and putting down the Lombard rebellion, and then crossing the Alps again and invading Saxony. Surprised by the speed of Charlemagne's movements, no one dared oppose him. Saxons "from every region" appeared at the sources of the Lippe near Paderborn and swore to become Christians and to recognize the rule of Charlemagne and the Franks.

They promised their fatherland (*patria*) as a pledge of their subjugation. This formulation was used in the royal annals composed at Charlemagne's court and discloses the following intent: if the Saxons kept their oaths of loyalty, they would remain subordinate to the Franks. If they did not keep their oaths, then the Franks would have the right to enter the Saxon lands and treat them as traitors.

The sources then report the foundation of a Frankish stronghold named "Karlsburg." There has been a great deal of discussion concerning the importance of the Karlsburg, which has been identified with Paderborn. It is notable that this place was named after him, following the model of Constantinople (the city of Constantine), showing that Charlemagne saw himself in the tradition of the first Christian emperor. In the following year, Charlemagne summoned a large royal assembly to Paderborn. This was a novelty since these assemblies normally took place in Frankish territory. Obviously Charlemagne believed that the Saxons had been subjugated once and for all. Many of them were baptized and the consecration of a church of the Redeemer was intended to open the systematic missionary activity in this area. Charlemagne felt so confident at this point that he responded readily to the appeal by the Muslim governor of Saragossa to support him against the emir of Cordoba.

Charlemagne actually appeared in Spain in the following year, but by that time the situation there had already changed dramatically. He marched to Saragossa; however, his ally no longer ruled there. Since Charlemagne could not take the city, he turned back. During his return march, Charlemagne razed the defenses of the city of Pamplona which led the infuriated Christian Basques to attack and wipe out the Frankish rearguard in the Pyrenees. This battle was made famous by the twelfth-century *Song of Roland* in which the commander of the Breton march named Hruodland or Roland played a leading role. Contemporary writers by contrast did not consider this an event worth of transfiguration. Instead, the royal annalists close to court refrained from discussing this incident which, tellingly, was first mentioned again during the reign of Charlemagne's son Louis the Pious. This defeat was embarrassing in itself for the Frankish ruler, but even more so as he had suffered the defeat in the context of a campaign against the heathen Arabs. Charlemagne had not coped with the most solemn task of a Christian ruler, namely the expansion and protection of the faith.

To make matters worse the Saxons once more took advantage of Charlemagne's absence to rebel, this time under the leadership of the Westphalian noble Widukind who had fled the previous year to the king of Denmark. The Saxons destroyed the Karlsburg, which had been erected with such great ambition, and even advanced as far as Deutz on the Rhine. There they took booty and destroyed many churches. "After years of an apparently unstoppable rise, the limits of Carolingian power suddenly became apparent" (R. Schieffer). Thus, 778 is rightly understood as the first year of crisis in Charlemagne's reign. It is interesting that it was at this time that Charlemagne recalled the memory of the Merovingians, the old royal family of the Franks, which had been overthrown by his father. During his absence, Charlemagne's third wife Hildegard had born twin boys. Along with Charles and Carloman, his elder sons by this marriage, and Pippin the Hunchback, these twins were intended to secure the future of the dynasty. Charlemagne gave significant names to his newborn sons: Louis (Clovis) and Lothar (Clothar). With these names Charlemagne made a connection to two famous Merovingians: Clovis I who had expanded the kingdom southwards into Aquitaine and Clothar I who had defeated the Saxons. In this manner, Charlemagne evoked the victorious days of the Merovingians in order to overcome the present crisis of his realm and to secure the loyalty of those Franks who might have lost heart. Contemporaries, however, may have already seen it as a bad omen for the war against the Saxons that little Lothar died soon after his birth.

Of course, Charlemagne also reacted militarily to these difficult circumstances. He heard of the Saxon successes as soon as he reached Auxerre and immediately sent troops to the Rhine. The Saxons withdrew to the region of the Lahn. However, they were caught and defeated on the Eder near Leisa. Their retreat route shows that the Saxons plundered the entire right bank of the Rhine up to Koblenz. Even the monks at Fulda had carried the relics of Saint Boniface over the Rhon mountains to safety. According to Hans-Dietrich Kahl, it was this rebellion which transformed the war against the Saxons into the gruesome event that has gone down in history. Through their rebellion and their attacks on Frankish territory, the Saxons, some of whom had become Christians and sworn oaths of loyalty to the Frankish king in the years before, provided the Franks with a formal justification for still harsher actions.

In 779, Charlemagne assembled his army at Düren and then crossed the Rhine at Lippeham (at the mouth of the Lippe?). There was a pitched battle at Bocholt that ended in victory for Charlemagne. After this, the way into Saxony lay open. According to the royal annals, all of the Westphalians were taken prisoner, which meant unconditional surrender. Charlemagne moved farther along the Weser and the Eastphalians swore oaths of loyalty to him, and had to give hostages as well. The Franks once more believed that they had defeated the Saxons completely because in the following year they tried to organize and divide the land according to their own ecclesiastical and secular notions. A contemporary annalist reported that the Saxons had surrendered and Charlemagne had then divided the territory among bishops, priests, and abbots so that they could baptize and preach. He received freemen as well as half-free (*liti*) as hostages. This report in all its brevity gives an important reason as to why the Saxons were able to maintain their intense resistance. Their struggle was supported not only by the nobles who might be inclined toward compromise because of their familial and other ties with the Frankish kingdom, but also, and above all, by the majority of the free and half-free population. When these classes also appeared ready to obey, Charlemagne was content and refrained in 781 from going to Saxony himself.

In 782, Charlemagne held an assembly at the sources of the Lippe at which all of the Saxons and even messengers of the Danish king Sigifried are reported to have appeared. Widukind was the only one who stayed away. Charlemagne went so far as to appoint several Saxon nobles as counts as a reward for their loyalty. He then returned to Frankish territory. But Charlemagne soon received reports of Slavic attacks on Thuringians and Saxons. In response, the king wanted to send a mixed Frankish-Saxon force to deal with the invaders. This combined with his appointment of Saxon counts indicates clearly that Charlemagne regarded Saxony as an established part of his empire. But at this point, large numbers of Saxons rebelled yet again under the leadership of Widukind. There was a battle on the north side of the Süntel mountains. The Frankish troops who had been sent out shortly before against the Slavs were defeated because of dissension among their commanders. Indeed, the Franks were killed almost to a man. Several counts and even Charlemagne's chamberlain and his marshal were among the dead. All the successes achieved in Saxony up to this point were reduced to nothing.

Responding to the seriousness of the situation, Charlemagne himself pushed forward with his men on forced marches toward the Weser. The Saxons assembled at the mouth of the Aler, surrendered, and handed over the rebels. According to the official account, 4,500 of them were executed. Widukind alone managed to escape to the Danes. There has been a great deal of discussion about the so-called bloodbath of Verden and it clearly shows the brutality of contemporary warfare even if the number "4,500" was greatly exaggerated by the royal annals. The notice that part of the Saxon population was deported in 782 fits within the context of the reports of more fierce and gruesome actions taken by the Franks. Charlemagne's reaction shows how surprised he was by the renewed rebellion of the Saxons. He believed that he had incorporated this territory within his kingdom, and now he had been forced personally to end the largest Saxon rebellion since the beginning of hostilities against them.

It was at this time that Charlemagne issued the notorious *Capitulatio de partibus Saxoniae* in which the death penalty was threatened for refusing baptism, for destroying churches, for plots against Christians, for breaking an oath to the king, and for violations of the requirements to pay tithes and to fast. We are dealing here with a harsh law of occupation although not all of the requirements were as draconian as they appear at first glance. Thus, for example, archaeological evidence indicates that cremation, which was penalized with death because it violated Christian burial practice, was hardly practiced any more in Saxony by the second half of the eighth century. The practice of building burial mounds, which was most common among the Saxon nobles, was not subject to the death penalty. Charlemagne "ordered" the burial on church grounds without threatening any penalties. Nevertheless, the Saxon leadership was required to give up one visible symbol of rank in a non-Christian society. Cannibalism and human sacrifice were subject to the death penalty there as elsewhere. The same applied to murder and robbing churches. The death penalty was not imposed, however, on some customs from Saxon religion such as the veneration of natural sites and meals in honor of the gods. In judging these penalties, it is also important to keep in mind that traditional Saxon law, for its part, was very severe and included numerous penalties to life and limb.

In the end, the *Capitulatio* may have proven more of a hindrance to a long-lasting Christianization since Charlemagne used the Christian religion as a means of suppressing the local population. He saw the church more as a tool of government than an ally. The inhabitants of parishes were required to provide the material basis for their parish church. This way of thinking had more to do with taking booty and the rule of conquest than with missionary activity. As E. Schubert formulated it, "first the church offerings and then the church." How would the practical efforts of the responsible ecclesiastical officials be received in a territory where the division into missionary areas had begun only two years earlier? The priests assigned to this work did not have an enviable task. They first had to convince their parishes both to provide material support to the church in the form of tithes and to put servants at their disposal before they could begin to undertake their spiritual work. At the end of the eighth century, the clergy harshly criticized this missionary practice. The *Capitulatio* was at least consistent in that asylum in a church offered the only legal protection for those threatened with the death penalty for having committed one of the crimes noted above. "The death penalty can be set aside in such cases following the testimony of a priest if the guilty party has freely gone to a priest and has confessed his secret deeds and is willing to do penance for them." It is doubtful, however, whether the extraordinary status accorded to the clergy actually improved their acceptance among the Saxons, since the latter bore a heavy material burden for the provision and maintenance of parish churches.

Despite all the victories and measures taken, Charlemagne was at first unable to break Saxon resistance. He was forced to launch a massive military assault against Saxony in 783. At this time, he proceeded with a small Frankish force toward Detmold where he defeated the Saxons in one of the few pitched battles of this war. Admittedly, his victory there can not have been particularly conclusive because instead of advancing, he retreated to the fortified Paderborn where he gathered more troops. It was only at this point that the king truly went on the offensive. He pushed forward, north toward the Hase and again defeated the Saxons. Then Charlemagne headed east crossing the Weser and finally arriving at the Elbe River. At this point, he ended the campaign and returned to secure Frankish territory along the Rhine. He celebrated both Christmas and Easter at the palace of Herstal.

Joined by some Frisians, the Saxons tried one more time to make use of the opportunity provided by the king's absence and rebel. Once more, Charlemagne crossed the Rhine and waged war. At Petershagen (near Minden) he could go no further because the Weser was at the high watermark. Charlemagne therefore decided to proceed toward Eastphalia through Thuringia while his son Charles was supposed to hold down the West-phalians. Charlemagne reached the Elbe where he managed to reach an agreement with several Eastphalian groups, and then returned to Worms in Francia. In the meantime, his son Charles had defeated the Westphalians and also returned to Worms. A Frankish assembly there resolved that the king should spend the winter in Saxony. His presence in Saxon territory was probably meant as much to shake the feeling of security among his native opponents as to strengthen the loyalty of his supporters. Charle-magne also spared himself a long march in the following year. On the other hand, he was taking a great personal risk, which may have been minimized since he was wintering at the secure fortress of Eresburg. Indeed, he even had his fourth wife Fas-trada and his children come and celebrate Easter with him there. Charlemagne regularly sent out the troops who were stationed in and around Eresburg against the Saxons even in periods of bad weather. In the spring, Charlemagne held an assembly at Paderborn. His seven-year-old son Louis appeared there ac-companied by the levies from Aquitaine. Thus, Charlemagne concentrated the powers of his kingdom for the decisive struggle.

The king took his entire force through Saxon territory up to the Elbe without encountering any opposition because, as the imperial annals noted almost cynically, the roads were free. Charlemagne had broken the native resistance. Only Widukind and his son-in-law Abbio eluded the Frankish advance and headed north of the Elbe. Charlemagne tried to negotiate and offered a personal meeting. In view of the overwhelming Frank-ish strength, Widukind and Abbio were willing to compromise and accepted Charlemagne's offer to come to Francia, though they demanded that Frankish hostages be handed over to ensure their personal safety. After this condition had been met, Widukind and Abbio followed the Frankish king over the Rhine. They were baptized at Attigny on Christmas Day 785. Charlemagne acted as godfather and honored Widukind with rich gifts. In this situation, Charlemagne demonstrated his political instincts by offering Widukind the possibility of an honorable surrender rather than pursuing him to the bitter end. The Saxon leader was permitted to return to his own estates and may have been given a high office in the Frankish hierarchy of offices as many of his fellow nobles had been before him. He is also reported to have rendered services to the Christian faith; for example, he founded the church at Enger where he may have been buried. His own myth grew independently. In later centuries his resistance against the (Christian) Franks was glorified, while on the other hand he was honored as a saint.

Widukind's baptism appeared to be the final fanfare of the Frankish victory. The royal annals reported somewhat prematurely that "all of Saxony had been conquered" (*et tunc tota Saxonia subiugata est*). Charlemagne also shared this view as is clear from his request to Pope Hadrian to have all Christians give prayers of thanks for the defeat of the Saxons. One can easily imagine the high spirits that followed thirteen years of bloody conflict. Charlemagne had brought this long-running battle to a (temporary) end due not least to his own personal commitment.

Charlemagne used the period of quiet in the north-east to turn to affairs in the south-east of his kingdom. Here, he would not be as generous toward the Bavarian duke Tassilo III as he had been toward the Saxon Widukind. Tassilo, who was Charlemagne's cousin on his mother's side, was not simply the administrator of the Bavarian duchy, he ruled this territory like a king.

He controlled the Bavarian church and held synods. He founded monasteries and provided them with extensive properties. In addition, he made efforts to spread the faith, especially in nearby Carinthia. In this manner, he fulfilled a more imperial task. Above all, he carried on his own foreign policy and maintained good relations with the neighboring powers. His wife Liutbirg was the daughter of the Lombard king Desiderius. Arichis, the prince of Benevento, was his brother-in-law. His cousin on his father's side Hildegard had been married to Charlemagne since 771 and thus guaranteed good relations with the Frankish king. Tassilo even succeeded in having the pope lift his son and future heir Theodo from the baptismal font in 772. His political position was thereby recognized by the highest moral authority in the West—apparently with Charlemagne's consent.

When Hildegard died in 783 relations between the two cousins visibly deteriorated. In 784 the first military clash took place in the Alps. In 787, Charlemagne finally invaded Bavaria with three armies. Tassilo submitted on the Lechfeld, swore an oath of loyalty, and received his duchy from the king as a fief. As security he gave twelve important men plus his son Theodo as hostages. One year later Tassilo appeared in Ingelheim where his famous, thoroughly discussed show trial took place. While the duke stayed with him, Charlemagne seized his family and his treasure and was therefore able to isolate him and take him prisoner without any danger.

The trial began. Bavarians loyal to the king appeared as prosecutors and charged the duke with breaking his oath of loyalty. He was accused of having established contacts with the pagan Avars who lived to the east of Bavaria. A further charge brought against Tassilo was that, twenty-five years earlier during Pippin's campaign in Aquitaine in 763, he had left the Frankish army without permission and was therefore guilty of *harisliz*, that is desertion. This act long since past could not seriously have been grounds for a sentence since Charlemagne and Tassilo had had closer relations in the meantime. It is also by no means certain that the other charges against him were justified in whole or even in part. In any event, until 787 Tassilo had ruled Bavaria in the manner of a king and might well have felt entitled to maintain contacts with the Avars. He might also have felt himself in the right in breaking an oath that he had been forced to make under duress. But if this had been the case he would not have appeared in Ingelheim but would instead have stayed at home. From his own point of view, and according to everything we know of the facts concerning his sentencing, it is most likely that Tassilo was not guilty. Nevertheless, he was condemned to lifetime confinement in a monastery and Bavaria thus fell to Charlemagne. Soon after, Charlemagne headed to Regensburg where he maintained his headquarters for several years and subjugated the land to his rule.

With Bavaria, the Franks also acquired a new and apparently powerful neighbor. The Avars, who had originally come from central Asia, had established a large kingdom during the sixth century in the Hungarian plain. These mounted fighters had continually disturbed their neighbors to the west and south, plundered them, and forced them to pay tribute. They had even successfully attacked the Byzantine empire on several occasions. In the eighth century, their power and ability to expand had gradually weakened. Nevertheless, they still played an important role on the central-European stage. In 788, the Avars invaded Italy and Bavaria. Perhaps Tassilo had really called on them, or perhaps they simply wished to take advantage of the unstable situation that developed after Tassilo was deposed.

Three years later, after he had secured his position in Bavaria, Charlemagne undertook his first Avar campaign. The Frankish army advanced toward the Enns River while the Avars retreated, avoiding battle. As a consequence, the campaign was basically unsuccessful. In order to deal better with the Avar military tactics, in 792 Charlemagne had a movable bridge constructed that could be carried along the Danube by ship and which facilitated repeated crossings of the river. At the same time, he attempted to build a Rhine–Main–Danube canal that would connect the two focal points in the north and south of his kingdom. This ambitious project failed, however, as it proved impossible to overcome the logistical difficulties.

Charlemagne did not let this deter him. While Charlemagne himself campaigned against the Saxons in 795, he issued orders for his son Pippin of Italy, the Bavarian prefect Gerold, and Margrave Eric of Friuli to fight the Avars. The latter were weakened by internal dissension so that Eric succeeded in reaching the Avar "ring fortresses" which lay in the Puszta plain near the Raab, and in taking the main ring. In 796, Pippin also managed to advance to the ring fortresses and he accepted the surrender of the Avar ruler. At this time, the victors obtained an immeasurable treasure consisting of the booty and tribute collected during hundreds of years of Avar rule. The greater part of the booty was divided among the nobles or granted to the church. Pope Leo III, whose election announcement reached Aachen at about the same time as the Avar treasure, received particularly rich gifts.

What was happening at this point on the Saxon front? After 785, there were several years of calm which Charlemagne had used to acquire Bavaria. The Saxons appeared to have come to terms with Frankish rule and even took part in Charlemagne's campaigns, for example against the Avars in 791. But when this campaign failed, the Saxons took this as the signal for a renewed rebellion. This failure seriously damaged Charlemagne's reputation as an invincible general. The Saxons' belief in the superiority of the Christian God was shaken, since the Avars who until recently had, like them, been pagan infidels and probably still were in their hearts, were not Christians.

These conflicts focused on northern Saxony in the Wigmodia between the lower Weser and the lower Elbe, and in the Bardengau and the area north of the Elbe called Northalbingia. Soon the former Frankish successes appeared to have been lost. In 793, a large Frankish force was destroyed at the mouth of the Weser. Charlemagne concealed the extent of the losses but cancelled a planned campaign against the Avars concentrating instead on the construction of a canal between Rednitz and Altmühl. This canal would certainly have shortened substantially the distance between the two trouble spots of his kingdom, namely the Saxon and Avar lands. However, this effort failed in the face of constant rain. When further bad news arrived from Saxony, Charlemagne retreated.

Charlemagne only renewed his campaign against the Saxons after Easter. Two armies campaigned against Saxon territory. The first, under Charlemagne's personal command, took the direct route. The second army under the command of his son Charles went by way of Cologne. The Saxons gathered at Sintfeld south of Paderborn. However, they avoided battle against their overpowering opponents who had them fenced in on two sides. They surrendered instead. However, in 795 they rebelled yet again along the usual lines and Charlemagne responded by heading north from Mainz. This time he reached the Elbe and the Saxons surrendered one more time. The following year

Charlemagne invaded again. In 797, he pushed north all the way to the North Sea coast near Hadeln and again accepted the surrender of what was supposed be the entire Saxon people. After other duties called him back to Francia, Charlemagne held an assembly at Aachen. Here, he issued the second Saxon capitulary, the *Capitulare Saxonicum*. He granted to the Westphalians, the Enger, and the Eastphalians the right to participate in law-making and thereby made them equal to all of the other peoples in his realm. It is likely that he rewarded the Saxons from the south, whom he had attacked first and who in the meantime had remained loyal to him, while the Saxon groups from the north were excluded.

It is not surprising that the *Capitulare Saxonicum* did not succeed in pacifying all the Saxon lands. As a result, Charlemagne again advanced into Saxony in mid-November 797 in order to winter there and bring order to the land. He established a camp south of Höxter in a place which Charlemagne called *Heristelle*. But the Saxons did not remain quiet, with the northerners revolting in 798. Charlemagne allied himself with the Abodrites and achieved further military successes so that the northerners surrendered and handed over hostages. In 799 he met in Paderborn with Pope Leo III who had fled from Rome, while his son Charles received the promised hostages from the northerners. After his imperial coronation in 800, Charles had the laws of all of his peoples written down. This included the Saxon law, the *Lex Saxonum*. Despite this manifestation of his power, however, in 804 Charlemagne was again forced to intervene in Saxony. At that time, Charlemagne had the population of Wigmodien, in the area of modern Bremen, and the people living north of the Elbe deported. He left the land on the other side of the river to his old allies the Abodrites.

The Expansion of the Frankish Kingdom in the East

The conquest of the Saxons was finally sealed, after an unimaginably long time even considering contemporary conditions. Charlemagne had had to dedicate thirty years of his life to
this task, a period of time that was longer than the reigns of
most medieval rulers. He had first crossed the borders of Saxony and destroyed the Irminsul when he was 24. He was 56, an
age that very few of his contemporaries ever reached, when he
finally defeated the Saxons utterly. Why did this struggle last so
long? Why were the Saxons, who could not match the Franks in
any area, able to resist for such a long time? The most important
reason was probably their political fragmentation. There was
no central power with which the Franks could have negotiated a
lasting treaty. There was no capital city whose capture could
have broken the resistance of the entire nation. There was no
king or duke whose capture would have rendered his people
helpless. In short, the apparent backwardness of the Saxons was
their strength. The countless surrenders, oaths of loyalty, and
hostages bound only some of the Saxon groups or peoples, never
the whole Saxon people as Charlemagne and the Franks might
have believed. Thus, their successes quickly evaporated as each
succeeding year a new group of Saxons rebelled and, after some
initial successes, perhaps carried with them some of those who
had previously been subjugated. Nevertheless, the Saxons could
never hope to achieve a military victory because the Frankish
power and technical military superiority were simply too great.
The pacification of the Saxons in this long and bloody war had
tested Charlemagne and the Franks to their utmost.

Looking back, Einhard interpreted the final inclusion of the
Saxons within the Frankish kingdom as a peace agreement "that
the Saxons would renounce their pagan gods and native religious practices, would accept the Christian sacraments, and

would join together with the Franks as one people." In fact, the serious changes in Saxony were not limited to the religious sphere. They lost their own institutions, which had strengthened their community, their heathen practices, and their rudimentary political organization. The country was oppressed by the conquerors' imposition of the Christian faith, along with the accompanying ecclesiastical administrative structure, as well as by the Frankish comital administrative system. Numerous confiscations provided for both ecclesiastical and secular office holders.

The king also intervened in the social structure by appointing native counts. A Saxon noble who became a count could generally improve his social status, and at the very least maintain it. Other Saxon nobles who maintained their hostility to the Franks must have been anxious about their status. One example of a successful accommodation to the new situation is Hessi, who in 775 was the leader of the Eastphalians. He entered Frankish service, became a count, and increased his wealth. Hessi's daughter, as we learn in passing, had to travel constantly in order to administer the properties she had inherited from him. Charlemagne's *Lex Saxonum* increased the social distance between the nobles and the rest of the population. The numerous deportations which Charlemagne ordered must also not be forgotten. These deportations shook the social fabric of Saxon society, and that is without considering the suffering of those who were directly affected. The Franks probably introduced the entirely new organizational principle of large estates, especially since both the church and the king participated alongside the secular nobles in this process. The establishment of bishoprics during the last years of the conflict, and particularly during the first years after that, had a tremendous impact on settlement patterns. There were now new central places with an entirely different architecture, consisting mainly of imposing stone churches. Thus, the subjugation of the Saxons by the Franks led to changes in all aspects of life whose dramatic and drastic nature cannot be overestimated.

V

CHARLEMAGNE, THE PAPACY, AND THE BYZANTINE EMPEROR

Thanks to his foreign policy successes, shortly before his imperial coronation Charlemagne was the most powerful Christian ruler in the world—apart from the east Roman emperor who had his seat at Constantinople (Byzantium). The east Roman empire stood within the unbroken tradition of the *Imperium Romanum* that had disappeared in the West in 476. As a result, Constantinople claimed at least spiritual leadership in the contemporary Christian world. All of the Germanic rulers of the West had acknowledged this position since none of them had claimed the imperial title until now. They had just called themselves kings. The disruption of the old power structure caused by Charlemagne's rise, which was made explicit by his imperial coronation, played an important role in his relationship with Byzantium. In particular, the papacy was affected since it maintained a special relationship with both of these powers.

Politically, the east Roman empire had always maintained a presence in the West thanks to Justinian's conquest of Italy,

North Africa, and southern Spain. These conquests were lost gradually one after the other to the Visigoths, the Lombards, and above all the Arabs. By the eighth century, Byzantine territory in the West had shrunk to a few bases along the Dalmatian and Italian coasts. These outposts included Venice, Naples, Amalfi, and the southern tips of the Calabrian and Apulian peninsulas. The most important possessions were Sicily and the exarchate of Ravenna, which included the city of Ravenna and the surrounding territory. They were connected by a narrow strip of land over the Apennines to the Byzantine duchy of Rome. The exarch, who bore the high-ranking Byzantine title of *patricius*, was the most important representative of the emperor in the West, acting as a type of vice-emperor, and was also responsible for Rome.

According to this constitutional arrangement, the popes had, until the first half of the eighth century, acknowledged, at least in principle, the emperor as their overlord. This was clear, for example, in the popes' practice of announcing their elections to the emperor. In the city of Rome itself, however, the popes were able to ward off the competition posed by the Byzantine imperial officials because the population of the eternal city, particularly the city's aristocracy, preferred to subordinate themselves to their own bishop rather than a foreign imperial officer. In addition, the popes were often members of the city's aristocracy. This animosity toward the eastern power increased as a result of struggles over high taxes imposed on the city. The relationship between the papacy and Constantinople visibly deteriorated when Emperor Leo III (717–741) introduced a harsh change in church policy by forbidding the veneration of icons (iconoclasm) while the pope held on to this practice. There had been similar struggles between Rome and Constantinople before, but two additional factors led to a final estrangement during the first half of the eighth century. First, the emperor deprived the pope of his ecclesiastical jurisdiction over the territories in the Balkan peninsula, which belonged to the empire, and in southern Italy, where he also confiscated several wealthy estates belonging to the Roman church. However, the emperor's actual power did not match this autocratic behavior. Secondly, the wars against the Arabs prevented the emperor from protecting the pope and the city of Rome from Lombard military expansion as he once had done. It was for this reason that Pope Gregory III turned for aid in 738/39 to the Frankish mayor of the palace Charles Martel, though in vain on this occasion.

In the end, the emperor was no longer able to maintain his most important base in Italy. The Lombards conquered the exarchate of Ravenna in 751. The same year, Charles Martel's son Pippin was elevated as king of the Franks with the help of the pope. These events marked the emergence of the alliance between the pope and the Frankish king, as discussed earlier. This alliance culminated in the establishment of Pippin as the *patricius Romanorum* and the transfer of Ravenna to papal control after it had been conquered from the Lombards by Pippin. The protest made by a Byzantine embassy was ignored. However, Pippin did not keep all the promises he had made in 754. He had promised large parts of the Lombard kingdom to the pope, yet now he stopped short of conquering them. Stephen II could still be pleased, however, that his relationship with the Franks had enabled him to strengthen the position of the papacy both against its old enemies the Lombards, and its old overlord the Byzantine emperor. Fear of the former's expansionist force and the latter's demands continued to determine papal policy.

Popes Paul I and Constantine (II) took into account the changed balance of power. They reported their elections in 757 and 767 to the Frankish king, something that had previously only been done with respect to the emperor. Paul rightly considered the Frankish king the only one who could protect him from a Byzantine attack on Rome. On the other side, the popes maintained their traditional link with Byzantium as is demonstrated by their continued dating of documents at Rome according to the imperial formula and by the minting of imperial gold coins. But the pressure that Rome faced from the Lombard kings in the following period forced Hadrian again to seek aid from the Frankish kingdom. Here, Charlemagne had become the undisputed ruler. As we have seen, however, he did not intervene in Italy without a degree of self-interest, and he brought the Lombard kingdom under his own rule. During the decisive siege of Pavia, he appeared early in 774 at Rome to celebrate Easter there. According to his biographer, Pope Hadrian was startled by this visit. On the one hand, Charlemagne was his ally. On the other hand, this speedy intervention in Italy also posed a danger to the political independence of the papacy. Despite this, or perhaps because of this, the pope received him with all of the honor that protocol demanded for an exarch or *patricius*.

Up to this point, neither Charlemagne nor his father Pippin had used the title *patricius Romanorum* to which they were entitled. It was only the popes who used this form of address in their letters to the Frankish kings. Now, Charlemagne was made welcome as a *patricius*. Unlike the exarch in earlier periods, however, he was not allowed to spend the night in the city itself, but instead had to find quarters outside the city of St. Peter. The pope no longer tolerated any secular rulers beside him. Additionally, Charlemagne had to give an oath of security at the tomb of Saint Peter even before Easter. He took this opportunity to renew the promise made by his father to Pope Stephen II in

754 at Quierzy, namely the donation of Pippin. The pope again saw the possibility of gaining further territories in central Italy. However, Charlemagne, like his father, did not keep his word in this matter. After the victory over the Lombards, only unimportant territories were conceded to the pope. His rule was contested even in the exarchate. The pope's episcopal brother, the archbishop of Ravenna, insisted on his independence at the expense of the papacy and at times sought close relations with the Franks.

As the ruler of the greater part of Italy and as the *rex Francorum et Langobardorum*, Charlemagne now began to use the title *patricius Romanorum*. From the point of view of the pope, this rank had until then meant that the Frankish kings had an obligation to protect the Roman church on behalf of the papal see. Now, Charlemagne ruled as king in the immediate neighborhood of the eternal city, and the title of *patricius* served to reinforce his claims to rule. This change of meaning certainly did not escape Hadrian's notice since he was very concerned to maintain his independence. It was during Hadrian's pontificate that the name of the Byzantine emperor finally disappeared from papal documents and coins. This action posed a clear challenge to the Byzantines. Despite the *de facto* rule of the pope in the city of Rome, according to the Byzantines, the city was still officially subordinate to the emperor in Constantinople. The pope's efforts to obtain independence in secular affairs did not exclude the Franks, his close allies and helpers. This connection was expressed in the so-called Donation of Constantine, a forgery created at the papal court at that time conceding rule of the western provinces of the Roman empire to the pope.

The conquest of the Lombard kingdom not only brought the Frankish kingdom closer to Rome, it also completely transformed the previously good relationship of the Franks with Constantinople. Already in 757, Charlemagne's father Pippin had approached the emperor in order to establish a pact of friendship although he refused to hand back the exarchate of Ravenna which belonged legally to the east Roman empire. The Byzantine return embassy may have brought imperial recognition of Pippin's elevation as *patricius* by the pope. In the following years both sides even pursued a marriage project: the emperor's son was to marry Pippin's daughter Gisela.

After the conquest of the Lombard kingdom by Charlemagne, however, Desiderius' son and co-king Adelchis fled to Constantinople. He received the title of *patricius* from the emperor. In Byzantine eyes, this placed Adelchis on par with the Frankish king, which was clearly a provocation directed against Charlemagne. In the fall of 775, an alliance was probably drawn up between the Byzantines and the Lombard dukes of Benevento, Spoleto, Friuli, and Tuscany whose goal was to drive the Franks from Italy and to place Adelchis on his father's throne. Rome was to return to its obedience to the emperor. Pope Hadrian learned of these plans and informed Charlemagne by letter. The latter appeared immediately in northern Italy and broke the rebellion in Friuli. He did not continue against the other dukes and also did not go to Rome despite a request from the pope that he do so. Nevertheless, Charlemagne's position in Lombardy was secure because the Byzantines did not intervene and Adelchis remained safe in far-off Constantinople. In the following years it was the pope himself who disturbed the peace. In 778, Hadrian launched offensive attacks by the papacy and conquered Terracina. This territory belonged to the duke of Naples and therefore to the Byzantine empire. Out of fear of a Byzantine reaction, Hadrian again tried to convince Charlemagne to undertake an offensive. But the Frankish ruler was constrained at this time by his Spanish adventure and by a Saxon revolt. There were also more important worries at Constantinople than dealing with the pope.

Charlemagne only appeared at Rome three years later at Easter in 781, and it was not just for the sake of prayer (*orationis causa*). The political ties between the pope and the Frankish king were consolidated at this time. On Easter Monday, the pope anointed and crowned Charlemagne's younger sons Pippin and Louis as kings. Charlemagne intended that Louis would rule the Aquitanians and Pippin the Lombards. By acting as godfather, Hadrian forged a strong spiritual bond of *compaternitas* between the Roman bishop and the Frankish king, just as in Pippin's time. In addition, the remaining problems concerning the Donation of Pippin were resolved. The pope received income and territory in Tuscany and the duchy of Spoleto, but gave up his demands for the fulfillment of the other clauses, specifically rule over all of Tuscany and Spoleto. Charlemagne proved himself to be the stronger and had only given away very little, despite the fact that the pope acceded to his wishes in another area. Hadrian took a stand against Tassilo of Bavaria who until then had always maintained good relations with Rome. A joint Frankish–papal embassy traveled to the duke in order to remind him of his obligations toward the king. Tassilo only deigned to appear before Charlemagne in August of that same year at Worms and, at the very least, acknowledged his formal membership in the Frankish realm.

Hadrian's actions in regard to the Donation of Pippin and the Bavarian question demonstrate his willingness to cooperate, but Charlemagne did not return the favor as expected. The pope had hoped that Franks would intervene in southern Italy in order to further militarily papal claims against the east Roman emperor. Instead, Charlemagne concluded an alliance with Byzantium in 781 that was to be secured by the marriage of Charlemagne's daughter Rotrud with the young emperor Constantine VI. Empress Irene had ruled as regent for her minor son since 780. At this time she was confronted with Arab attacks in Asia Minor and needed peaceful conditions in the West. It was probably for this reason that she was willing to recognize the exceptionally powerful position of the Franks in Italy including their protection of the city of Rome and the papacy. The Franks could believe at this time that they had all but achieved equality of status with the venerable east Roman empire. From Hadrian's point of view, this could at least be understood as an end of the Byzantine threat to Rome. It was only the Byzantines who gained little from this agreement, since in early 781 the governor of Sicily revolted against the empress and Irene was forced to send troops to the West after all.

A few years later, Charlemagne decided to intervene militarily in southern Italy. In doing so he was pursuing his own interests far more than the pope's. As a Lombard center, the principality of Benevento had become a real threat not only to Rome but also to the Franks themselves. Arichis of Benevento used the title *princeps*, and like Tassilo of Bavaria, he considered himself to be an independent ruler. Also like Tassilo, he was a son-in-law of the last Lombard king Desiderius and consequently a brother-in-law of the pretender Adelchis who lived in Constantinople. In March 787, Charlemagne invaded the principality and Arichis soon stopped resisting. He swore an oath to acknowledge Charlemagne's overlordship and handed over a number of hostages including his son Grimoald. In view of this success, Charlemagne may have thought that he was no longer dependent on his alliance with Byzantium. When an imperial embassy arrived to escort his daughter to the emperor at Constantinople, he refused to hand Rotrud over.

With this unprecedented provocation against the leading ruler of the Christian world and the campaign against the duke of Benevento, Charlemagne forced both parties into an alliance directed against the Franks. In fact, Arichis formed an alliance with Byzantium that same year, and acknowledged Byzantine overlordship in return for territorial concessions. In addition, Empress Irene now activated the Lombard king Adelchis, who had long been living in exile in Constantinople, and sent him to southern Italy where a Byzantine army was being assembled. This time, Charlemagne was aided by a providential event. Arichis died in August 787 at Benevento. The heir of this principality was his son Grimoald who, at that time, was Charlemagne's hostage. Against the pope's advice, Charlemagne let him go home. Grimoald thanked him for it the following year when, together with the duke of Spoleto, he defeated the Byzantine troops. Although Grimoald later renewed relations with Byzantium, the empire had had to abandon its great ambitions as had Adelchis who spent the rest of his life in Constantinople.

The true reason for Charlemagne's politically rather unwise break with Byzantium may be sought in his disappointed expectations. In contrast to his hopes, the empire continued to treat the Frankish ruler like a subordinate barbarian king. The marriage agreement had not changed anything in this regard since foreign marriages were not unusual for a Byzantine emperor. Constantine VI's grandmother was a Khazar princess, a member of a nomadic people from the northern Caucasus, most of whom were not even Christians. From the east Roman point of view, it was entirely reasonable that when in 787 the emperor called for an ecumenical council in Nicaea he invited the pope to send a delegation but not the Franks. It was suddenly clear to Charlemagne that all of his military successes and his political alliance with Byzantium would never give him equal standing with the ancient empire. He, the most powerful king in the western Christian world, had to wait for the decisions of the council like some minor Anglo-Saxon king and then accept them obediently. Charlemagne was no longer willing to accept this situation and broke off relations with Byzantium.

The Council of Nicaea, however, pursued a goal that was of universal not simply imperial interest. Constantine VI and Irene reintroduced the veneration of icons and thereby removed a theological controversy that had split the church for decades. Pope Hadrian welcomed this decision and sent his legates to Nicaea. He does not appear to have been troubled by Constantine's disregard for the Franks, as this fell within a long-established behavioral pattern that had been common since the days of Constantine the Great. The emperor was the only secular ruler who was permitted to participate in decisions concerning the church as a whole. As patriarch of the West, it was the pope who acted in effect as the representative of the Franks. After all, only a few years earlier the Franks had asked for ecclesiastical law and liturgical texts in order to reform their church and to set it on the correct path. Was the successor of Saint Peter supposed to take these barbarians into consideration and permit their participation in an ecumenical council? So Charlemagne's argument was directed indirectly at the pope as well. Since there had been no Frankish bishops at the council, it could not be considered ecumenical. Furthermore, the Franks had always supported the correct position concerning the veneration of icons.

1. Charlemagne lays siege to the walled city of Pamplona. Relief from a shrine to Charlemagne at Aachen, thirteenth century. Bildarchiv Foto Marburg.

. Drawing made of a mosaic visible in the *triclinium* of the Lateran Palace until the eighteenth century. Saint Peter presents a pallium to Pope Leo III and a standard to Charlemagne. Rome, Biblioteca Vaticana.

3. Farmworkers in the four seasons. Illuminated manuscript, early ninth century. Vienna, Österreichische Nationalbibliothek.

4. Gold coin of Charlemagne from Ingelheim. Landesamt für Denkmalpflege Rheinland-Pfalz, Abt. Archäologische Denkmalpflege, Kaiserpfalz Ingelheim, M. Schlotterbeck 2001

5. Carolingian cavalry and footsoldiers. "Psalterium
Aureum" (Book of the Psalms), end of the ninth century.
Stiftsbibliothek St. Gallen.

6. Charlemagne's monogram.
Modena, Biblioteca Capitolare.

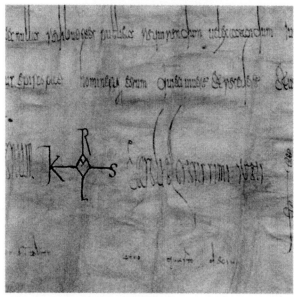

7. Charlemagne with his son Pippin and a scribe. Lupus von Ferrières,
Liber Legum. Modena, Biblioteca Capitolare.

8. The so-called Throne of Charlemagne, between 760 and 825.
Aachen Cathedral, gallery of the Carolingian octagon.
Photo: Ann Münchow.

It took years before the Frankish court received a translation of the council's acts which had been completed at Rome after the pope had approved the results. Charlemagne hardened his position and took the opportunity to stress his political jurisdiction in Gaul, Germania, and Italy. The court theologians of the Frankish king expounded his position in the so-called *Libri Carolini*. The results of the Council of Nicaea as well as its changed position regarding iconoclasm were to be rejected. Hadrian pressed for the acceptance of these decisions while Charlemagne only refrained from publishing the *Libri Carolini*. In the course of these negotiations, the pope suggested a compromise at the expense of the emperor and to his own benefit. He wanted to declare Constantine VI a heretic despite his return to faith unless he made amends for the injustices done by his great-grandfather Leo III, following the prohibition of the veneration of icons. The emperor was to restore the possessions and rights that had been taken from the Roman church at that time. "It could not be clearer that the Roman church had turned away from the East, from the Greek church, and from the Roman empire, and toward the Franks, or more accurately toward a papal territorial lordship whose existence was protected and guarantied by the Franks. A renewed unity with the Greeks in matters of faith was of little importance so long as the Franks protected Rome's autonomy and the Greeks disregarded it." (Classen)

Within this context, however, the pope had to accept that Charlemagne emphasized his control over the church in a manner that resembled very closely that of the Byzantine emperor. In 794, Charlemagne summoned a council to Frankfurt. It was not unusual for the Frankish bishops to gather around their king. However, Charlemagne now ruled the former Lombard kingdom as well. As a consequence, the old Roman provinces of Gaul, Germania, and Italy were all represented at the council. In addition, there were representatives of the Anglo-Saxon church from Britain and even legates from the pope. As had been true at Nicaea, the most important theme was heresy. A new doctrine concerning the true nature of Christ had developed in Spain. Jesus was to be understood as the adopted rather than as the bodily son of God. The Franks and the papacy firmly opposed this view and the council at Frankfurt took its stand accordingly. The delegates also discussed the Council of Nicaea with the result that its decisions were dismissed. Charlemagne thus visibly put the pope in his place. The pope's representatives supported these decisions despite the fact Hadrian himself held an entirely different view on the validity and effectiveness of the regulations set by the Council of Nicaea. Probably in order to save face, the pope finally confirmed neither the decisions of the Council of Nicaea or those of the Council of Frankfurt. Charlemagne had formally stressed his claim to equality with the emperor.

Pope Hadrian died on Christmas Day 795. Charlemagne genuinely mourned the loss of his long-time partner. Einhard reports that news of Hadrian's death moved Charlemagne to tears. Charlemagne had a black marble gravestone sent to St. Peter's on which one can still read a poem written by Alcuin, the head of Charlemagne's court school: "I shed tears for the father. I, Charles, had these verses written for him. I weep for you father my heartfelt love. I unite the names with shining titles: Hadrian and Charles, I a king, you a father. You who pray here and read these humble verses, speak: God show mercy and take pity on these two!" If Charlemagne had already insisted on his pre-eminent status to the esteemed Hadrian, he did so all the more with Hadrian's successor Leo III. Charlemagne left to him only the task of praying, while he wanted to protect the Roman church and defend Christians generally against heathens and unbelievers. Charlemagne wrote this to Leo III on the occasion of his victory over the pagan Avars in 796. This military and political success provided Charlemagne with the opportunity to remind the pope of the division of duties between the secular and ecclesiastical authorities. The victory over the Avars, who had once been feared as the scourge of Christendom, considerably increased the self-confidence at the Frankish court. Thus Alcuin, Charlemagne's learned advisor, described the realm on this occasion as an *imperiale regnum*, an imperial reign. It took only four more years for Charlemagne to establish true imperial rule in the West.

During the Frankish triumph over the Avars, Constantine VI cast his mother Irene from power in Byzantium. In 797, however, the empress succeeded in deposing her son and having him blinded so as to make him incapable of holding the throne. After this, she ruled in her own name. According to one report, a party in Byzantium, perhaps even the empress herself, offered the imperial title to Charlemagne in 798. These events certainly strengthened Charlemagne's resolve to pursue the highest secular honor at an opportune moment. The Roman rebellion against Leo III in 799 finally brought such an opportunity. Alcuin wrote to his lord: "Up to this point, three people have held the highest positions in the world. The first is the pope in Rome who holds the holy see as the vicar of Saint Peter prince of the apostles. The second is the imperial dignity and secular power of the second Rome. The third is the royal dignity to which you have been raised as leader of the Christian people through the mercy of our lord Jesus Christ. You are more powerful than the other two. You are more noble in your wisdom. You are more awe-inspiring in the dignity of your kingdom. The well-being of the churches of Christ rests on you alone." These lines mirror Charlemagne's increased self-confidence in those days. Without undue haste but with great purpose he pursued his goal of standing at the head of the Christian world not only in fact but in name as well.

Charlemagne's elevation as emperor on Christmas Day 800 was seen as a provocation in Byzantium. The important role played by the pope was taken especially badly. The crowning of the emperor in Constantinople by the patriarch was understood as a mere spiritual accessory to the purely secular act of elevating an emperor. Thus, the historian Theophanes caricatured the anointing of Charlemagne, which was not reported in the main western sources, as the extreme unction of someone dying rather than as the consecration of a ruler. This ridicule was intended, however, to obscure how deeply offended and how threatened they felt on the Bosporus. There had been many usurpations in the past and many anti-emperors had been raised in Italy, even at Rome. They had all been imperial subjects who had striven for control over the Byzantine empire. Now it was a barbarian who dared to grasp the Roman imperial dignity and the Byzantine court did not know what to expect. Did Charlemagne intend to attack the east Roman empire in order to capture Constantinople, the true capital of the Roman empire, and thereby take his usurpation to its logical conclusion? Since nothing of the kind occurred, Irene sent an embassy to the West in order to discover Charlemagne's intentions. Frankish and papal emissaries traveled to Constantinople with an answer. Possibly it was in this context that rumors arose about a marriage project between Charlemagne and Irene, rumors that lacked any basis in reality. Nevertheless, in the eyes of her opponents these rumors compromised the elderly empress, who chose to deal with the barbarian usurper rather than to fight him. Indeed, it is perhaps no coincidence that the empress was deposed at the end of October 802 while the western emissaries were still at her court.

The head of this conspiracy, the high official Nikephoros, ascended the throne. However, he too pursued negotiations. In the summer of 803, a new Byzantine embassy appeared before Charlemagne. He gave them a written outline for a peace agreement. Although the text of this document has not survived, it can be assumed that Charlemagne demanded acknowledgement as emperor. In terms of power politics, Charlemagne probably pursued continuation of the status quo. To Nikephoros, however, acknowledgement was out of the question and therefore he did not respond to his suggestion. However, Nikephoros did not consider this question of rank worth going to war over. Military conflict arose only out of tangible territorial interests. In Venice, which was subordinate to the Byzantine empire but enjoyed considerable autonomy, near civil war-like conditions arose. The various parties sought support either from the Byzantines or from the Franks. When Charlemagne formally incorporated Venice and Dalmatia into his empire in 806, Nikephoros could not stand for it. The result was a four-year-long war. The Frankish forces were superior on land while the Byzantines controlled the sea.

Neither side was able to gain a decisive advantage until 810. At this time, Nikephoros was planning a war against the Bulgarians who continually threatened his capital. He then sent emissaries to the Franks in order to bring the military conflict to an end. Charlemagne took this opportunity to resolve the question of Byzantine acknowledgement of his being emperor. In order to reach agreement on this point, he was even prepared to give up Venice. However when the Frankish envoys arrived at Constantinople, Nikephoros was already dead. He had fallen in battle against the Bulgarians in 811. His son-in-law and successor Michael I continued the negotiations and finally recognized Charlemagne as emperor. Within the context of the Byzantine conception of the fundamental superiority of their own empire as a continuation of the *Imperium Romanorum*, Michael interpreted Charlemagne's empire as a simple elevation in rank for a king who ruled numerous peoples. In order to emphasize this distinction, Michael added the Roman character to the official Byzantine imperial title. From now on, the ruler of the second Rome on the Bosporus was no longer simply "emperor" but "emperor of the Romans." In the summer of 812, however, Charlemagne was acclaimed emperor at Aachen by the Byzantine envoys. After twelve years he had reached his goal and received acknowledgement of his new title from Constantinople.

This external recognition of his status as emperor should not obscure that fact that Charlemagne had seen himself as emperor since Christmas Day 800. This became especially clear in the sphere of ecclesiastical politics which affected the East as well as the West. In Jerusalem, where Charlemagne could consider himself to be protector, a theological dispute broke out between Frankish and Greek monks. The Franks had made an addition to the credo stating that the Holy Spirit proceeded from the father *and* the Son (*ex patre filioque procedit*). Charlemagne initiated a council held at Aachen in 809 that resolved the conflict over the *filioque* clause. The way the decision was reached very much recalls the Frankfurt council in 794 concerning the veneration of icons. The Frankish synod called on the pope to agree to the addition to the credo. Leo III refused to do so since this would have disturbed the unity of the eastern and western churches. This demand demonstrated, however, the new sense of self-confidence among the Franks who even in ecclesiastical matters no longer wished to submit to the pope. Thus, despite the fact that the pope had the older form of the credo, as established by the Council of Nicaea in 381, written in Greek and Latin on both sides of the tomb of Saint Peter, the credo continued to be sung in the Frankish kingdom with the addition of the *filioque*.

Charlemagne had achieved a position in the western Christian world like no other ruler since the days of the west Roman emperors. He ruled as emperor in an empire that stretched from the English Channel to southern Italy and from the Elbe to beyond Pyrenees. The pope was politically subordinate to him and was not even in a position to decide in the ecclesiastical matters of the Franks. The Byzantine emperor acknowledged a barbarian ruler as an equal for the first time. Charlemagne even exchanged embassies with the far-off Arab caliphate in Baghdad thereby keeping in touch with the third great power in the Mediterranean region. One result of this relationship was Caliph Harun-al-Rashid's transfer of administrative control over the Holy Sepulcher to Charlemagne in 802. This act significantly increased the prestige of the western emperor. It was not the east Roman emperor, who for decades had been on the defensive against Islam, but the ruler of the West who became the protector of the Christians in the holy sites in Jerusalem. Charlemagne had led the Frankish kingdom to a unique high point of power.

VI

RULING THE EMPIRE

In addition to its foreign policy dimensions, Charlemagne's elevation as emperor also had important effects on his exercise of lordship within his kingdom. In Charlemagne's view, this newly acquired title was not merely a formality, but rather changed qualitatively his status within the realm. Nothing makes this clearer than Charlemagne's effort in 802 to require the entire population of the realm swear an oath of loyalty—on the *nomen Caesaris*, the imperial title. This was the second general oath of allegiance since 789, one year after the fall of Duke Tassilo of Bavaria. At that time, *infideles homines*, disloyal people, had excused themselves for their revolt by stating that they had never sworn an oath of loyalty to the king and were therefore not obligated to him. This excuse was no longer to be accepted. From this time on all freemen who had reached thirteen years of age were required to swear loyalty to the emperor.

In 802, the emperor went a step beyond what had taken place in 789 by defining more strictly the flexible concept of fidelity. In the past, the view was taken that to fulfill one's oath of loyalty it was sufficient not to threaten the life of the ruler or to summon any enemies into the kingdom. Now Charlemagne demanded more from his subjects. All people were expected to keep God's commandments, to respect all the emperor's possessions, to acknowledge his protection over the churches and the weak, especially widows and orphans, and finally to obey imperial commands. These demands seem somewhat peculiar to us today because some of them have nothing to do with the business of state and others appear to be self-evident. However, in Charlemagne's time they were not and this demonstrates how little rulership had developed and how difficult it must have been to enforce state authority in the modern sense.

The other element of his demands stems from Charlemagne's conception of himself as a Christian king. He sought to fulfill the rules that were set forth in the Fürstenspiegel treatises, which were written during his time and elaborated the ideal conduct for princes. Alcuin himself repeatedly reminded Charlemagne of the most important task of the king, *correctio*, that is leading his subjects. These views ultimately originated in Augustine's work and were inspired by the admonitions to the Israelite kings described in the Old Testament. *De XII abusivis saeculi* (Concerning the Twelve Vices of the World)—attributed to the church father Cyprian and written in Ireland about 700—was an exceptionally influential work, in which the obligation of the king for *correctio* was stressed. He must not indulge in unjustified oppression of his subjects, but must give a just judgment without considering who was being judged. His obligations included the protection of the church, widows, and orphans, the fight against theft and other crimes, care for the poor, seeking good counsel and appointing good officers, as well as combating heresy. These obligations repeatedly shine through in Charlemagne's internal political measures.

The difficulties that a medieval ruler could have in enforcing his authority can be seen, for example, in Aquitaine. In 781, Charlemagne invested his son Louis, his third son from his marriage with Hildegard, as sub-king there. During one of his father's visits, Louis only presented him with an appropriate gift after receiving a direct order to do so. When asked why, Louis answered that he found himself in a difficult position because his magnates, without exception, strove for their own advantage. On the one hand, they neglected public lands, and on the other they sought to transform them into private possessions. Louis was ruler only in name. Charlemagne's reaction to this seemingly scandalous situation was surprisingly mild. He reasserted royal control over the former royal fiscal properties but refrained from taking any punitive measures. He probably did not want to accuse the Aquitanian nobles of deliberately damaging the royal properties because this might have driven them into open rebellion. Although they had not rebelled in any way, but rather—at least in their own view—were loyal, their egoism endangered the king's position. Disciplining them over the long term was as difficult in its own way as warfare against declared enemies. Charlemagne's demand that the population of the empire leave imperial fiscal property untouched was an effort to force people, particularly the nobility, to recognize the special status of the ruler without setting out on the path toward confrontation.

All in all, the necessity of the general oath demonstrates how weakly developed lordly authority was within the realm. Thoughout his reign Charlemagne worked to increase his authority. Documentary evidence for his efforts survives in numerous capitularies—texts which were divided into chapters—which should be classified somewhere between laws and decrees. In 779, soon after the first serious crisis of his reign, following his failed campaign into Spain in 778 and a setback in Saxony, Charlemagne issued at Herstal the most important capitulary of the early period of his rule. The problem of loyalty had already been dealt with. Here, Charlemagne banned so-called guilds and sworn associations. The members of these associations created bonds of loyalty among themselves that might be given preference in a conflict with the king.

Shortly after another crisis—namely the rebellion by Hard-rad and the removal of Duke Tassilo of Bavaria—Charlemagne issued the next important capitulary, the so-called *Admonitio generalis* or General Admonition of 789. Under the influence of the learned Anglo-Saxon Alcuin of York, Charlemagne was depicted in this capitulary as the ruler of the Christian people, impressing on all his subjects obligations to the Church such as keeping Sunday holy. There are also some significant regulations which can be understood as suggesting a general oath of loyalty. Charlemagne prohibited perjury, especially when oaths were sworn over the gospels, over an altar, or over relics, as well as when numerous people swore the same oath. The last point is most relevant to a general oath of loyalty since this was sworn in groups before royal officials.

Charlemagne's next important act as a lawmaker took place during the important Synod of Frankfurt in 794. In its ecclesiastical decisions, this council reacted in a very particular manner and contrary to the east Roman Council of Nicaea against Adoptionism, a belief which had arisen in Spain that Christ had only been a man filled by God's Holy Spirit. Its secular decisions are clearly directed against internal weaknesses of the empire.

In 792/93, Charlemagne's oldest son, Pippin the Hunchback, had revolted against his father. Pippin, who had been practically excluded from the succession, found numerous supporters in the high nobility. It seems likely that there were Bavarians within this group who wished to free Tassilo from the monastery. The rebellion failed and Pippin spent the remainder of his life behind monastery walls. Shortly thereafter, Tassilo appeared publicly for the last time at Frankfurt in order to give up any claims to rule over Bavaria in his name or in the name of his descendants. It was only then that Charlemagne could really regard his lordship over Bavaria as secure, since the "show trial" of 788 had not been a legitimate basis for deposing the duke. Establishing his lordship within the empire was more difficult than one might have imagined given Charlemagne's numerous successes in foreign affairs.

Against this background, the imperial coronation not only meant increasing power and above all respect, but also a serious threat. The Frankish nobility was resourceful when it came to evading the ruler's authority. Thus, it is easy to imagine the next impending threat. Those, like the participants in Hardrad's conspiracy of 786, who argued that they were not bound to the king because they had not sworn an oath, could now easily justify their further disloyalty by claiming that they had sworn an oath to the king but not to the emperor. Thus, from Charlemagne's point of view, the oath of 802 became a necessity. The broadened concept of fidelity, as sketched out above, was intended to enforce the ruler's demands. Many of Charlemagne's goals to strengthen the loyalty of his subjects looked good on parchment but could never be put into practice—at least not over the long term. Instead, Charlemagne, like all his predecessors, had to buy the loyalty of his magnates in the usual way—with gifts and other demonstrations of favor, and above all by assigning them important responsibilities.

In contrast to his predecessors, however, Charlemagne was not satisfied with this practice. According to his self-conception, he sought to be a ruler like the emperors of antiquity or the Byzantine emperors of his own time. Their word was law and, at least in theory, they did not have to waste their time on willful magnates. Charlemagne's incredible tenacity is evident from the fact that he never lost sight of his goals and continually issued capitularies expressing his views despite the considerable difficulties and resistance that he faced. And indeed, just by having his directives written down, the Frankish ruler imitated his great Roman models.

In 802, Charlemagne not only made the population of the empire swear an oath, he also engaged in intense legislative activity shortly after his imperial coronation which amounted to something like a "program of imperial government." (François/Louis Ganshof). The *Lorsch Annals* sum up his activity in the following manner: "And in the month of October, the emperor assembled a general synod at the named place [Aachen] and asked the bishops along with the priests and deans to read all of the canons which had been adopted by the synod, as well as the decretals of the popes. He ordered that these decrees be translated before all the bishops, priests, and deans. In a similar manner, he assembled all the monks and abbots who were present at the synod and asked them to read the rule of the holy father Benedict which was translated for all the abbots and monks [. . .] Then the emperor himself assembled all dukes, counts, and other Christians along with the legal scholars and had all the laws of the empire read out and translated so that each man heard his own law. He ordered that improvements be made wherever necessary, and that the improved law be written down to enable the judges to make their decisions on the basis of written law and not accept any gifts. So all people, rich and poor alike, were to have justice."

Let us take a closer look at the secular aspects of this legislation. Charlemagne either re-edited or recorded for the first time Frankish, Frisian, Saxon, and Thuringian codes of law. He made additions to the laws of the Bavarians and Alemanni in the form of capitularies. He conceded a certain amount of independence to subjugated peoples, although the influence of Frankish law is clearly perceptible. Recording laws which up to this point had been orally transmitted by various peoples had a significant impact on their traditions. Not only did Charlemagne want to give a formal structure to the legal system of his empire and thus make it easier to govern, but he also wanted to strengthen his authority throughout the empire. Therefore, for example, it is not surprising that Charlemagne was still renowned as a law-giver in thirteenth-century Saxony.

However, these laws had to be implemented. To this end, in order to structure and organize these parts of the realm thoroughly, the administrative system of counties was exported, even into newly conquered territories. Just like the *comes* of the Merovingian period, the Carolingian count commanded the military contingent from his district and presided at court. Both functions offered considerable economic possibilities since parts of the fines were due to the count, and his decisive role in the army provided him with the opportunity to deprive free farmers of their independence. However, it was not possible to extend this system of counties to cover the entire empire because, since the Merovingian period, there had been numerous ecclesiastical immunities (areas free from royal jurisdiction but guaranteed by the ruler), as well as allodial noble lordships. Even the counts, whom Charlemagne considered his officials, sought to become independent of the ruler's control. Furthermore, the ruler was not completely independent when appointing the counts since he had to take make allowances for hereditary claims and the local balance of power. In addition, the distances between the imperial court and certain counties were sometimes very large, which in itself made it difficult to translate decisions from the central authority to the countryside.

Nevertheless, Charlemagne strove to effect a positive change in these conditions. He intervened in the judicial system to improve the position of the poor and the powerless. During the Carolingian period, public life was sometimes characterized by extreme violence. Criminals were pursued with only limited success because of the rudimentary administrative system which lacked, among other things, a police force. Taking the law into one's own hands and vendettas were the order of the day. At least in theory, Charlemagne limited these problems by the obligation that the wronged accept reparations, if offered, from the guilty party. This usually occurred in a legal case. The counts or their representatives held court in the name of the king and passed sentences, while experienced legal representatives interpreted the law. These men had been chosen on an ad hoc basis until Charlemagne required that each judicial district have regular *scabini*, or lay judges. North of the Alps, these men belonged to the ranks of the richer land owners, whereas in Italy they were professional notaries. At the same time, the obligation of all freemen to attend court was limited to three times a year. In addition, Charlemagne established the office of the so-called reprimandary witnesses who were required to bring crimes to the attention of the court if the victims did not do so themselves.

Despite his good intentions, it is doubtful whether Charlemagne was able to succeed in bringing about a universal application of his policies or achieving his stated goal of having justice prevail more frequently. Alcuin aptly describes the difficulties which even the great Charlemagne could not overcome: "I am convinced of the king's good will, unfortunately there are more people who stand in the way than support him."

One means of binding the office holders more closely to the ruler at least in a personal manner was through vassalage, i.e. through the feudal system. The word *vassus* is Celtic in origin and designates a ruler's subordinates. During the Merovingian period, dependent free people as well as the unfree were called *vassi*. Dependent free people, or their ancestors, probably entered this state of dependence because of economic necessity or due to pressure from their future liege lords. This dependence was symbolized by the *commendatio*. This meant that the subordinate put his hands in the hands of his liege and promised him *servitium vel obsequium*, service and obedience. On the other side, the liege was obliged to support those who commended themselves to him. Frequently, this meant that the liege granted his subordinate a plot of land to farm. This formalized relationship of dependence eventually made its way into the upper social classes, while its origin remained in the public consciousness for a long time. Indeed, Charlemagne had humiliated Duke Tassilo to the extreme by requiring him in 787 to become his vassal and to accept Bavaria from him as a fief.

Even if it was a means of humiliating Tassilo, this event contributed decisively to the fact that vassalage became socially acceptable at the end of the eighth and early ninth century. Men, who in their youth had been brought up at the royal court and had become vassals there, frequently rose to be counts. These *vassi dominici*, the vassals of the ruler (the king), were of course nobles whose fathers generally were already counts themselves. If the ruler trusted them, after years of loyal service he would offer each of these men their father's county or another. They remained his vassals and thus very closely bound to him. Over time, the two functions blended into one so that it became normal for a count or other official also to be a vassal of the king. This rise in social prestige brought with it changes in the nature of vassality, especially the obligations of the vassals. They were no longer expected to provide *servitium vel obsequium*, but rather *consilium et auxilium*, counsel and aid. In other words, the ties gradually loosened and broadened the flexibility and position of the vassals toward their liege lords.

Another means of improving the administration of the empire was to establish an intermediate authority whose task was to oversee local officials. In order to accomplish this task, the king normally dispatched the *missi dominici*, the king's envoys. According to the *Annals of Lorsch*, in 802 Charlemagne decisively altered this practice. Charlemagne no longer entrusted poorer vassals from the court with these missions, but, "rather chose archbishops, and other bishops, and abbots, and dukes, and counts in his realm who had no need to take gifts from the innocent. And he sent them throughout the empire so that the churches, widows and orphans, the poor, and all the people could have justice." The royal agents usually went out in pairs— one ecclesiastical and one secular official—and traveled a yearly circuit of numerous counties and bishoprics, "in order to control and organize everything for the benefit of the king." (R. Schieffer). But their authority was largely dependent on their status and reputation which meant that even before 802 many of them had belonged to the high nobility just like the counts over whom they were supposed to exercise control. As a consequence, they were not open to bribery. However, even close associates of Charlemagne, such as the Bishop Theodulf of Orléans, were often faced with gifts while undertaking their duties and certainly did not turn them all down. In addition, friendships and relationships naturally led to conflicts of interest between the official obligations of the king's envoys and their personal goals. But Charlemagne was no idealist and he appears to have recognized these problems. In the "program for the imperial government" issued at Aachen, he insisted that all those who had complaints, whether Christian or heathen, stood under his protection, and that anyone who attacked such people, turned them into dependent servants, or sold them would face the death penalty. By its very existence, this rule shows the extent of the resistance to the ruler's intentions.

Only the ruler himself could properly control his officials. As a result, Charlemagne was almost always on the move. His court took up residence in various royal palaces in the countryside as well as in monasteries and episcopal sees. The royal palaces included old Merovingian sites such as Compiègne, Quierzy (north of Paris), and Attigny (near Rheims) which Charlemagne's father Pippin had also preferred. Charlemagne also brought new palaces into the spotlight which show that the empire's center of gravity had shifted eastwards. These palaces included Frankfurt, Ingelheim, Diedenhofen, Worms, and finally Aachen, which from 795 on served as Charlemagne's winter palace. Aachen was modeled after Ravenna and Pavia. One can only speculate on Charlemagne's choice of location since its advantages could certainly have been provided by many other places. Aachen did offer the advantage of the hot springs, in which the aging Charlemagne could swim, and the extensive forests to the west where he could pass his time hunting—the appropriate activity for nobles. In 801, Charlemagne had the statue of Theoderic the Great transported from Ravenna to Aachen. In doing so he tried to establish a link with the great king of the Goths—who like Charlemagne himself was a barbarian—and had ruled large parts of the former Roman empire.

The organization of the royal court was adopted from the Merovingians. However, the office of the mayor of the palace, which the Carolingians had used to deprive the Merovingian kings of their power, was abolished. Four court offices remained: the treasurer, the marshal, the seneschal, who was responsible both for feeding the household and for the administration of the imperial fisc, and the chamberlain who oversaw the administration of the court. The count of the palace participated in administering royal justice. The functions of the Merovingian chancery were transferred to the royal chapel. The chapel was originally the place where the *cappa*, the cloak, of the Frankish royal saint Martin was kept. The clerics who served there were therefore called *capellani*. Their head, who in later times was called archchaplain, oversaw the writing of royal charters and letters. The chapel was also used to store important documents. This is how it gave its name to all the clerics who served in the chapel.

In addition to the *missi dominici* were the imperial assemblies, regularly held by Charlemagne, which served to maintain the bonds between the ruler and his ecclesiastical and secular magnates. The theoretical work, *De ordine palatii* (On the Order of the Palace), composed by Archbishop Hincmar of Reims, notes that two imperial assemblies were to be held every year, a general assembly early in the year and a smaller one in the fall where only higher officers were to appear. At these assemblies projects for the coming year were discussed and planned. Charlemagne frequently did not hold these general assemblies until the summer. During the early years of his reign, these assemblies usually took place at Worms or Ingelheim. Later, most assemblies were held at Aachen. General problems such as the price of grain, monetary values, or simply the summoning of the army were often dealt with. However, these assemblies also involved juridical proceedings and the welcoming of foreign ambassadors. Occasionally, these assemblies also expanded into synods as was the case at Frankfurt in 794.

The royal estates were the material basis for royal rule. The fisc consisted of properties in the regions that would become Lotharingia and the area along the Mosel as well as Merovingian fiscal properties, especially in the Ile de France and in the area around Soissons. Around 800, Charlemagne had an account drawn up detailing the royal fisc throughout the empire, which meant everything down to the last wooden rake was listed including all the buildings, cattle, and an inventory of all royal properties. Only a small part of this effort has survived, but even so it provides us with our most important source for understanding the Carolingian agricultural economy. In this context the *Capitulare de Villis*—a detailed decree directed at the administrators of the royal fisc—must be mentioned. It contains regulations concerning the cultivation of fruit trees and vineyards, the care of forest lands through clearance and reforesting, the expansion of specifically designated crops, including cabbage and herbs, and the rearing of cattle and smaller animals, especially birds. The king demanded not only that the administrators deliver a precisely determined quantity of products from the royal estates, but also that an eventual surplus would be stored or sold, and these gains precisely recorded.

Charlemagne wanted the administration of the royal fisc to deal with the smallest of details, and may have been hindered here as in the administration of the entire empire by the egoism of his officials. This edict too may also have been in issued in reaction to a crisis, namely the famine of 792/93.

Charlemagne sought to reform and reorganize in other areas as well. These efforts were particularly enduring as regards monetary policy. He asserted the exclusive right of the king to mint money so that all coins were minted either in royal mints or at least with royal permission. Building on his father Pippin's efforts, Charlemagne established a monetary standard that remained the basis for the currency for a very long time. One pound of silver produced 20 shillings which corresponded to 240 pennies. Twelve pennies or denarii had the same value as one shilling or solidus. This was only a unit to assist with calculations, as the shilling was usually not minted at all since it was of no use in the daily life of an agricultural economy. The only preserved gold solidus from Charlemagne's reign, which was recently discovered in an excavation at Ingelheim, was characteristically minted at Arles in Provence. Gold coins of somewhat lesser value are known from Italy. It is likely that production in the catchment area of the Mediterranean was centered at this time on long-distance trade and finance with the result that high value coins of this type could circulate.

Charlemagne's measures to reorganize the military service of free people, the *liberi homines*, must be understood within the context of his great military campaigns. The size of one's property was supposed to determine how often and how intensively one was called up for military service. These measures were necessary because in 805 a summons for military service in the area between the Seine and the Loire had failed on account of a famine. As a result, Charlemagne ordered that every tenant with three to five so-called hides (homesteads), as well as the holders of fiefs, were required to serve against the enemy. A tenant of two hides had to join with another in the same position. The one who was more capable of fighting had to go into battle, while the other provided him with economic support. The same rules applied to two freemen, one of whom possessed two hides and the other one hide. Men with only one hide had to join in groups of three. The one who could most easily be spared was to be equipped by the other two. Those who possessed half a hide were grouped together so that five could support a sixth who went on campaign. Charlemagne also issued similar regulations for those who did not have any land but had a certain amount of cash. Just a few years later, the size of property that obliged one to service in the army was raised from three to four hides.

These regulations were long seen as evidence for the economic decline of freemen. They could no longer bear the high costs entailed by military service because Frankish warfare over the second half of the eighth century came to be based on armored cavalry. The free farmers could not afford the horses or the expensive armor. However, the fact that even during the ninth century the majority of the Frankish army consisted of foot soldiers casts doubt on this explanation. Furthermore, the assumption of a general military obligation seems too modern. It is based on the notion that a societal order based on freedom and equality had lasted from the dim and distant past up to the late eighth century. But, circumstances were very different from what used to be believed by earlier scholars. As early as the sixth century, the magnates and their followers formed the backbone of Merovingian military forces. The numerous civil wars of the second half of the seventh and first half of the eighth centuries were waged exclusively by the noble military retinues. There never was a general obligation of military service up to the time of Charlemagne. Indeed, it was Charlemagne himself who introduced this obligation and had to consider the conditions of poorer freemen, as we have seen, in order to recruit them at all.

These regulations were probably necessary because the Carolingian empire had reached the limits of its fullest possible expansion around 800. During his wars of conquest, Charlemagne had largely been able to rely on the nobility and their military retinues. Small farmers, who would have been more or less forced to go into foreign regions, would of necessity have left their fields untended for an indeterminate length of time. As a result they would have been of little use. The nobility could afford to participate in these expeditions, especially since they received a disproportionate share of the booty. Now, however, the Frankish empire itself fell victim to plunderers on the prowl. From the first decades of the ninth century, the Vikings plagued the Frankish coasts and began to advance inland in search of booty. The defensive war that was necessary to resist them was of no interest to the nobles: there was nothing to gain. It is therefore not surprising that *defensio patriae*, 'home defense,' is frequently mentioned in the context of freemen's military service. Only those freemen who were directly affected by the attacks were willing to face the invaders, while the nobles, who held properties in numerous provinces, could avoid these problems.

In addition to his efforts regarding the economy, administration, and the army, Charlemagne was also concerned with education and scholarship. His court was home to the most important scholars of the western Christian world who, at least at first, were not only recruited from within his empire. These included the Anglo-Saxon Alcuin, the Visigoth Theodulf of

Orléans, the Lombards Paulinus of Aquilea and Paul the Deacon, and the Irishman Dungal. They had all benefited from exceptional educations in their homelands. Obviously at first no Frank could compete with them. Charlemagne's empire, in fact, was suffering from a near educational emergency, a result of the decline during the late Merovingian period which had had exceptionally disastrous effects on education and scholarship. It was only gradually that Franks came to join this elite, foremost among them Einhard, the author of the *Vita Karoli magni.*

Within this circle, the view probably developed that not only their own works but every written text was to be measured by classical standards. This was not an end in itself but above all to serve as a better understanding of Christian faith and the proper course of religious services. Regional developments in the liturgy conflicted with the unity of the cult. Even more importantly, the Latin language, in which all texts were written, was breaking apart and gradually developing into the various romance languages. As a consequence, there were problems of comprehension which were the basis of difficulties in establishing a unified liturgy.

The reform of the church was as much of interest to Charlemagne as the secular organization of his empire. He was able to use the preliminary work of Boniface and Chrodegang of Metz as a basis for his own efforts. In the process Charlemagne made use of authoritative works in this process which indicate the importance of Rome for Frankish church reform. As early as 774, Charlemagne asked Pope Hadrian for an anthology of church law which had been produced in the sixth century by Dionysius Exiguus and which Hadrian himself had expanded. This *Dionysio-Hadriana* was used enthusiastically in the Frankish kingdom. Likewise, the king asked Rome for a sacramentary (a mass book) from Pope Gregory the Great, which was to serve as the basis for a unified liturgy. Furthermore, soon after 787, Charlemagne obtained a copy of the rule of Benedict of Nursia, that is a copy of the original which at that time must still have been at Monte Casino. The rule of Saint Benedict, however, was closely tied to Roman monasticism and may even be traced back all the way to Pope Gregory the Great. Even if numerous other works followed, these three texts formed the foundation of Charlemagne's effort to reform the church.

One of the central concepts of reform was concern that the correct text, which was to ensure the correct and unified organization of ecclesiastical life in the entire Frankish empire, was used. Charlemagne clearly stressed this point to his bishops and abbots in the circular letter *De litteris colendis* (On the Care of Studies). The most important precondition was the establishment of schools in episcopal churches to ensure a basic education. Charlemagne's maxim stated that "good action is better than proper knowledge, but action derives from knowledge." Clerics and monks were educated at these schools and were the only ones to put these books to good use, make copies of them and starting to circulate them. In order to avoid the earlier problems of comprehension, Charlemagne insisted on the use of classical Latin. Thus, the West saw the development of a pure language, which was used almost exclusively by the learned, and from which the romance languages grew increasingly distinct. A new script even developed in the western part of the empire, the so-called caroline minuscule. The standardization of the script was an important prerequisite for the diffusion both of the new ideas and of old texts. Alcuin's contribution in this effort was the most important. At the request of Charlemagne, he edited the Bible, eliminated errors and barbarisms from it and put it down in caroline minuscule. This text would become authoritative although, like other Carolingian texts, not universally accepted.

Charlemagne not only promoted education, but also called on his subjects to obey Christian teachings and to turn away completely from paganism. He did so most notably in the *Admonitio generalis* of 789 in which he emulated the biblical king Josiah, who was always concerned about the order of his realm. Charlemagne insisted that clerics and monks live a Christian life so that they could do justice to their roles as the models and shepherds of their flocks. Once Carloman and Pippin, under Boniface's influence, had taken action against secularized clerics. But they acted only half-heartedly, since they needed the political support of these clerics. Only very cautiously did they try to separate the secular and ecclesiastical functions of bishops. Charlemagne continued this cautious approach, although he did stress the need to maintain canonical regulations and venerable traditions more than his predecessors. "Bishops were supposed to spend as much of their time as possible at their sees and in their dioceses; and one bishop should never hold more than one see. Their primary concern should be for the clergy and pastoral care ... Diocesan synods were established for the improvement of pastoral care, to educate and oversee the clergy. The bishops were supposed to keep an eye on everything, everywhere at all times: what the priests taught, how they celebrated the service, and whether they lived a proper life. Bishops should regularly visit their parishes, check on the lives of the Christians living there and confirm the adolescents." (A. Angenendt)

Anyone given such responsibility also needed to be controlled. This was the role of the archbishops. Charlemagne did not force the re-establishment of the metropolitan organization, but introduced it gradually. During the early years of Charlemagne's reign, there was only one archbishop, Wilchar of Sens, who had replaced Chrodegang of Metz. It was only after his death in 786/87 that the number of archbishops began to increase until we reach a total of twenty-one metropolitans listed in Charlemagne's will of 811. In his capitularies, particularly the *Admonitio generalis*, Charlemagne already assumed a working metropolitan system. This system was only curbed by Charlemagne himself, as he continued to hold imperial synods. He thus counteracted the right of archbishops to summon the bishops of their own church provinces. The ruler was not supposed to name bishops and abbots, but Charlemagne nevertheless continued to do so at his discretion. On occasion, Charlemagne even left a see vacant in order to use its properties for his own purposes. The true head of the Frankish church, now as before, remained the king.

The internal organization of the Frankish empire under Charlemagne was widely marked by a considerable divergence between desire and reality. According to modern scholars, Charlemagne's empire after 800 encompassed approximately 1 million square kilometers with 180 dioceses (excluding the emerging papal state), 700 monasteries, 750 royal estates (*fisci*), which enclosed some 150 palaces with 25 fully erected residences, 150 administrative districts in Italy, 20 in Frankish Spain, and 500 in Gaul and east of the Rhine. This unimaginably large empire was probably only "governable" because far fewer demands were made on the state by contemporaries than today. But Charlemagne himself was not satisfied with this situation. On the contrary, he continually strove to implement his far-reaching policies. But the reality in his empire looked different as he himself probably realized. In 813, at the end of his reign, Charlemagne ordered as many as five synods to be held (in

Arles, Rheims, Mainz, Chalon, Tours), which were supposed to deal with the shortcomings. Charlemagne failed because of the individual interests of the nobles, of which he was undoubtedly aware. But he could not restrict them effectively as he needed them for the administration of his empire. It was the traditional right of the nobility to serve the king in a distinguished position. The king had to consider these claims since his great conquests would have been impossible without the support of the nobility. As early as 802, Alcuin assessed the reform efforts of his lord in the following manner: "I am certain of the good intention of our lord and emperor and that he seeks to order everything in the realm granted to him by God according to what is just. However, I am also certain that he has more followers who seek to undermine justice than who seek to support it, that is more *praedatores*, robbers, of justice than its *praedicatores*, preachers, that there are more who seek their own advantage than those who look after God's advantage." Only a few of Charlemagne's undertakings for the organization of the empire proved to be lasting, with the result that the last years of Charlemagne's reign can be described as an era of decay and crisis (Ganshof). But perhaps this impression stems from Charlemagne's own high expectations of the effectiveness of his "state," which he put down in his capitularies. In the end, it was only his educational reforms that had wide-ranging effects and laid the foundations for a standardized culture of the Latin West.

VII

CHARLEMAGNE'S FAMILY AND THE ARRANGEMENT OF HIS SUCCESSION

One of the decisive reasons for the success of the early Carolingians was the fact that they could rely on their own family, particularly its male members. Neither Pippin II, nor Charles Martel, nor Pippin the Younger's sons revolted against them. It is true that Charles Martel and Pippin the Younger had conflicts with other relatives before succeeding in establishing themselves as the sole rulers of the Frankish kingdom. The same is true of Charlemagne who was only spared a military confrontation with his brother Carloman because of the latter's death. In contrast to his predecessors, Charlemagne had to cope with a revolt by one of his own sons. Einhard describes this event in the following manner: "He had a son named Pippin by a concubine who was handsome but a hunchback. While his father was fighting against the Huns (Avars), he spent the winter in Bavaria pretending to be ill. There, he made a pact against his father with several Frankish magnates who had misled him with idle hopes of kingship. After the discovery of this plot and the condemnation of the conspirators, Charlemagne had Pippin shorn and placed in the monastery of Prüm according to the king's will, so that he might lead a life dedicated to God." Supposedly, Pippin's goal was royal rule. But as the son of a concubine did he have any legal claim? As will become clear, Einhard's short and rather veiled report leads to the general theme of "family" and "succession."

First we will look at Charlemagne's relationships with women, specifically with his wives and concubines. Sometime after 763, Charlemagne had an intimate relationship with a noble girl named Himiltrud who gave birth to Pippin the Hunchback. In 770, following his mother's advice, Charlemagne married a daughter of the Lombard king Desiderius whose name remains unknown. As discussed earlier, Pope Stephen III opposed this marriage because he maintained that Charlemagne was already legally married. Therefore, in contrast to Einhard's account, Pippin was not the son of a concubine but rather the product of a legal marriage, at least from the point of view of the pope at the time. This did not keep Charlemagne from dismissing Himiltrud. Her skeleton was recently discovered in the monastery of Nivelles and an investigation has determined that she died long after 770. The Lombard princess was sent back to her father for political reasons after less than a year. Charlemagne married again soon after, perhaps as early as 771. This time he married Hildegard, who was descended on her mother's side from the dukes of Alemannia and was also closely related to Tassilo of Bavaria. Her father Gerold held extensive lands in Carloman's kingdom. Over the long term, this marriage was the most important politically for Charlemagne because it strengthened his position in the regions east of the Rhine. It was also the most important for the continuation of the dynasty because

Hildegard bore three sons who reached adulthood: Charles, Pippin, and Louis. In addition to this marriage, the king also had a relationship with a concubine who was presumably a noblewoman. Hildegard died at the end of April 783 shortly after the birth of her daughter who also died a few weeks later. That same year, Charlemagne married Fastrada, who was a daughter of the East Frankish count named Radulf, at Worms. According to Einhard, she exercised a great deal of political influence. It is reported that, as with Hardrad before, it was her harsh behavior that drove her stepson Pippin the Hunchback to rebel. After Fastrada's death in 794, Charlemagne married an Alemannic woman named Liutgard. She died in 800 before the imperial coronation. After this, Charlemagne did not marry again. The three concubines who are known to us came from unimportant if not unfree families. One of them came from the recently defeated Saxons.

Charlemagne's attitude toward women falls into a traditional pattern in his family as is clear from the examples of Charles Martel and Pippin II. Only Charlemagne's father Pippin followed church teachings in his marriage to Bertrada. Admittedly, Pippin once intended to divorce his wife but abandoned this plan after the pope's admonition. His laws concerning marriage also followed church teaching since he excluded illegitimate children from inheritance. By contrast, Charlemagne's own conduct flew in the face of Christian doctrine on marriage. His practice of keeping several women at the same time and his arbitrary separation from them stood in direct violation of church teaching. However, it was only after Charlemagne's death that anyone dared to criticize openly his way of life in this respect. A monk from Reichenau is supposed to have had a vision of Charlemagne suffering a gruesome penance for his fleshly sins despite his contribution to the defense of the faith and to leading the church. Like the Merovingian kings, Charlemagne lived a polygamous life in which relationships were not strictly defined in legal terms. He only contracted fully valid marriages with women who came from families that were more or less equal to his own. The marriages therefore also served the political function of binding these families closer to the ruling dynasty. And the relatives of Charlemagne's wives played correspondingly important roles at his court. Gerold, the brother of Hildegard, was even made prefect of Bavaria after Tassilo's deposition, so that in practical terms he took over the role of the former duke.

But as the case of Himiltrud demonstrates, even lawful wives were not immune from being dismissed. We know virtually nothing about her relatives, but we can certainly assume that a political connection with them was not nearly as important as the anticipated alliance with the Lombards. Charlemagne's marriage plans for his two younger sons also served to consolidate power since they were married relatively early to noblewomen from their sub-kingdoms of Italy and Aquitaine. It is impossible to explain why the eldest son Charles remained unmarried until his death in 811 at the age of almost forty, especially when compared to the behavior of his contemporaries. This probably did not correspond to the wishes of his father, as is indicated by the plan in 789 to marry Charles to the daughter of Offa, the Anglo-Saxon king of Mercia. This project failed because of Offa's desire to have Charlemagne's daughter Bertha marry his son and heir Ecfrith.

Charlemagne had other ideas and kept all his daughters unmarried under his own *munt*, that is his paternal authority. The marriage of one of his daughters would have enhanced her husband's and his family's status too much, not to mention the future claims of a grandson. Thus, Charlemagne strengthened the special status of his family and kept the nobility at a distance. Charlemagne was even cautious in his view of any link to the king of Mercia who, in comparison to the Frankish king, was a relatively unimportant ruler. Only in the case of the Byzantine emperor Constantine VI was Charlemagne willing to agree to the marriage to his daughter Rotrud. However, this plan was undone by the estrangement of the two empires. Even so, the projected union indicates that Einhard's assumption that Charlemagne loved his daughters so much that he could not bear to part with them and therefore kept them from marrying was not entirely true. In his efforts to keep his daughters from marrying specifically Frankish nobles, Charlemagne was following in the tradition of the Merovingian kings who frequently placed their unmarried daughters in convents. This attitude can also be seen in Charlemagne's successors.

Charlemagne allowed his eight daughters—three from Hildegard and the remaining five from his various concubines—to remain at court. He also took in the five daughters of his dead son Pippin. To later observers, this situation was scandalous since Charlemagne's daughters lived as man and wife with their lovers and had children. Alcuin warned one of his students against the princesses: "see that the crowned doves who fly about the rooms of the palace do not come to your window." Theodulf of Orléans reports that they took part in all important acts of royal representation, at festivals, banquets, and on the hunt. They accompanied their father to Rome in 800 and attended his coronation as emperor. It is possible that in Charlemagne's later years they exercised considerable political influence on their aged father and, in a fashion, collectively fulfilled the function of a queen. Charlemagne does not appear to have objected to their behavior or to the role they played. When Louis the Pious came to power in 814, he forced them to withdraw from court. However, he did so less out of outrage over their way of life than out of a desire to curb their influence.

The political importance of an early medieval queen should not underestimated. She was in charge of the court's administration and therefore participated in the decision as to where the court should stay. For example, Alcuin once asked Queen Liutgard where Charlemagne was planning to spend the winter. The queen was also in charge of the treasury and therefore controlled one of the important instruments of rule. In the ruler's absence, the queen usually acted for him while they maintained close contact. The only surviving personal letter from Charlemagne is addressed to Fastrada. In it, he tells her about his campaign against the Avars in 791 and a three-day fast for the success of their undertaking. She was asked to have the same done at the court in Regensburg. Charlemagne reported further on the military successes of her stepson Pippin of Italy against the Avars in which she was apparently very interested. At the same time, Charlemagne sent his youngest son Louis the Pious to her and entrusted him to her care. Louis had served for a short time in the campaign against the Avars. The queen, therefore, played an active part in the important political events of her day and assured that the court functioned smoothly in the absence of the ruler. Thus, it was not only as a husband but also as a ruler that Charlemagne complained at the end of his letter to Fastrada that he had not had any news from her since he left Regensburg.

At a very early date Charlemagne began training his sons for the succession. As early as 781, he elevated his younger sons from his marriage with Hildegard, Carloman and Louis, as

sub-kings of Italy and Aquitaine. On the occasion of his consecration by the pope, Carloman received the new name Pippin.
There were, therefore, now two Pippins in Charlemagne's family; Pippin of Italy in addition to to Pippin the Hunchback. One
might assume that this points to Charlemagne's efforts to thwart
the claim to the throne of his misshapen son. The new king of
Italy's change of name also may have been intended to recall the
friendly policies of his grandfather toward the papacy. In addition, it was this latter Pippin who had been adopted in 738 by
the Lombard king Liutprand. The name "Pippin" therefore
stood for the multiple relationships of the Franks with the
south. The oldest of Hildegard's sons, who had been named
after his father, together with his half-brother Pippin the
Hunchback was meant to be the heir to the original kingdom of
the Franks. When the father gradually moved away from his eldest son this drove Pippin the Hunchback into rebellion against
him in 792/93. As a result, Charles the Younger was found more
and more at his father's side or acting as his deputy in important
campaigns. In 789, he received part of Neustria to rule. However, it was not until 25 December 800, that is the day of the
imperial coronation, that Charles the Younger was anointed
and crowned as king by Pope Leo III.

In 806, Charlemagne decided on a final succession and put
it into writing, the *Divisio regnorum* or division of the kingdoms. This was promulgated in the form of a capitulary or law,
and was related to the measures that had already been taken.
Charles the Younger was to receive the entire Frankish core
region from the Loire to the Rhine along with the newly
acquired regions up to the Elbe and the Danube, whereas Pippin
was to receive Italy, which he already ruled, as well as Bavaria
and southern Alemannia. Aquitaine, as well as Septimania,

Provence, and parts of Burgundy were intended for Louis. Unlike earlier divisions, this time the Frankish core region was not to be divided. Charles the Younger was to have sole possession of the Carolingian family property in Austrasia, the old royal properties in Neustria, as well as the churches and monasteries that were closely linked with the Carolingian family in the two former sub-kingdoms. This is a clear sign that Charles the Younger was intended as his father's principal heir despite the fact that the territories of his brothers were not much smaller than his. All three of them received borderlands so that burden of defense against foreign enemies would be divided equally among them. Further expansion was not mentioned. In fact, the Frankish kingdom had long since reached its limits. All three brothers were entrusted with the general obligation to protect the Roman church, which is why all three were given crossings over the Alps. Even the pope joined this agreement. Einhard brought him a copy of the *Divisio*, which Leo III countersigned. The nobility also gave their consent and the entire population of the empire was made to swear to Charlemagne's order of division.

Charlemagne did not, however, content himself with the organization of his own succession. He was already thinking of the next generation. If any one of his sons should die, his kingdom should be divided equally between his two brothers. Charlemagne even set out the borders for the three possibilities. These divisions seem "strangely rationalistic" (P. Classen) since they did not take cognizance of geographical or historical conditions. Italy and Aquitaine, for example—two united kingdoms that had grown over time and whose independence Charlemagne himself had recognized by establishing his younger sons there— would have been divided. These plans put the grandchildren at a disadvantage since they would only have a chance with the explicit consent of the nobility. Both Pippin of Italy and Louis of Aquitaine already had sons whose rights of inheritance would have been limited in this manner. It was once thought that this preference for the older generation was an old Frankish custom. However, one should first consider the exceptional circumstances of 806.

It is characteristic that Charlemagne would have thought about how his sons would treat the next generation following his death: "Concerning our grandchildren, the sons of our aforementioned sons, those who have already been born or perhaps will be born, it pleases us to command that under no circumstances shall any of them be killed, mutilated, blinded, or shorn against his will without a legal investigation and trial . . ., rather we desire that they shall be respected by their fathers and uncles, and that they themselves shall obey them with the devotion appropriate for one who belongs to such a family." Such an obligation especially towards the uncles was necessary, since Charlemagne expected his grandchildren to stand behind their uncles in the line of succession. Speaking here was the father and uncle who could not get the monastic confinement of his eldest son and his nephews out of his mind. The reference to his grandsons' obligations toward his sons also served to ease his conscience, since Pippin the Hunchback had revolted against his father and Carloman's sons had been a severe danger to Charlemagne's rule. But, as Charlemagne himself knew best, this was only part of the truth since he had himself forced Pippin out of the line of succession and his nephews had been minor children.

This consideration of the grandchildren, nephews, and sons of the future rulers shows that other relatives besides the ruler's wives and children belonged to his family. First we should recall the exceptionally important role that Charlemagne's mother Bertrada played during his first years as ruler. She remained at his court until she died in July 783. Charlemagne's sister Gisela, who had once been intended by her father Pippin as a spouse for the Byzantine imperial heir, served as the abbess of the convent of Chelles, where under her tutelage an important historical work was composed. Charlemagne's uncle Bernard, who was an illegitimate son of Charles Martel, appeared as a commander in a campaign against the Lombards. He was probably even married to a noble Saxon woman. His children were welcome guests at court. Charlemagne was very close to his cousin Gundrada although she did not share his view of life. According to her brother Adalhard's biographer, Gundrada kept her virtue "in the midst of burning passions at court and the all-encompassing virile youth and beauty." Adalhard was brought up with Charlemagne at the court of his uncle Pippin. He supposedly left the court out of anger that Charlemagne divorced his Lombard wife. Later, however, he once more enjoyed the king's favor. He became abbot of Corbie and later founded the monastery of Corvey in his mother's Saxon homeland. Wala, another of Bernard's sons and a cousin of Charlemagne, played an important role at court. Both of these men lost their influential positions under Louis the Pious.

Charlemagne left one important question unanswered in his *Divisio regnorum*: which of his sons should succeed him as emperor? In contrast to the title to the Frankish kingdom, the empire was intrinsically indivisible. This had been at the heart of the difficulties with Byzantium following Charlemagne's elevation as emperor. The Franks had taken the view that there was no emperor in Constantinople; so it was legal to raise a new emperor, namely Charlemagne. Admittedly, Charlemagne's court was aware that this argument was not entirely sound. In fact, there were now two Roman emperors, a situation that was bearable so long as they did not recognize one another. It was for this reason that in 806 Charlemagne decided against naming his successor as emperor since before doing so he had to come to some agreement with the Byzantine emperor.

When the east Roman emperor recognized Charlemagne as his equal in 812, the western emperor could finally designate his official successor. However, Charles the Younger had died one year earlier and Pippin of Italy had died in 810. The only heir left was Louis of Aquitaine for whom Charlemagne apparently had less regard than for his elder sons. Following east Roman practice, Charlemagne made Louis co-emperor in September 813, without including the pope in the ceremony. After a joint prayer and a long admonition to care for his sisters, his half-brothers, and relatives, Charlemagne crowned him as emperor. Before this happened, extended councils with the magnates of the empire had been necessary in order to convince them to accept this seemingly natural succession. Apparently, there was opposition to Louis. This assumption is supported by the fact that Charlemagne had appointed his grandson Bernhard, the son of Pippin of Italy, as his father's successor in the former Lombard kingdom against the provisions issued in the *Divisio regnorum*. Charlemagne's cousins Adalhard and Wala, who were not among Louis' friends, were named as regents for the young king.

Charlemagne's private will of 811 was significantly different from his political decrees. He divided all his personal property, including all of his jewels, into three parts. Two of these were then further divided into twenty-one portions—the number of metropolitan sees of his empire. The remaining third was to be used for the support of the emperor until his death or his voluntary retreat from secular life. After his death, the items of daily life were also to come into it: vessels and tools made of ore, iron or precious metals, as well as weapons, clothing, and other household goods, whether valuable or not, hangings, coverings, carpets, felt and leather, and saddlebags. This third was to be divided into four parts. One quarter was to go to the metropolitan sees. The second quarter was to go to his sons and daughters and to the sons and daughters of his sons, who were to divide it as right and proper. Following "time-honored Christian custom," the third quarter was to be distributed among the poor. The last quarter was to be given to the palace servants. The court chapel received undivided possession of all its endowed goods. The books from his library were to be sold "for a good price" to those who were interested and the income was to be given to the poor. Charlemagne had begun a second will in which he intended to bequeath something to his children by his concubines. However, he died before he could complete it.

As was his wont during the last years of his reign, Charlemagne spent the winter of 813/14 at Aachen. According to Einhard, that autumn he hunted until the beginning of November in the area around his favorite palace. He was seized by a strong fever in January and had to take to bed. In order to defeat or at least to alleviate his illness, Charlemagne began to fast. He died on the morning of 28 January 814, the seventh day of his illness, at the age, according to Einhard, of 72 years. In fact he was only 66. After his body had been washed and arranged, he was buried the same day at the church of Saint Mary at Aachen. Einhard wrote that Charlemagne did not leave any instructions regarding his final resting place. This does not accord with the fact that shortly after his accession Charlemagne had arranged for a burial site at Saint-Denis. However, after forty years it is likely that no one in Aachen could or would remember this early plan. Charlemagne's daughters were certainly involved in this decision and perhaps wanted to anticipate their brother Louis the Pious, now the sole ruler. It would be wrong, however, to suggest that Charlemagne was buried with unusual haste, since it was not uncommon for someone to be buried on the same day that he died. Above his grave, which lay in the entrance hall of the church, a golden arch with his image and the following inscription was erected: "Here lies the body of Charles, the great and faithful emperor, who gloriously expanded the kingdom of the Franks and ruled for 47 years. He died as a seventy-year-old in the year of the Lord 814 in the seventh indiction, on the 28th of January."

VIII

EPILOGUE
HERO AND SAINT

The Afterlife of Charlemagne

The creation of myths around Charlemagne actually began during his own lifetime. The members of his so-called court school, especially Alcuin and Theodulf of Orléans, lavished the ruler with praise. In their panegyric poems they emphasized that his education, vision, and intelligence outshone everything. Another poet described Charlemagne as the "father of Europe" and the "venerable lighthouse of Europe." His death lead to an outpouring of grief. "From the rising of the sun to the shore of the sea where it sets all hearts are full of sorrow. Alas! The Franks, the Romans, and all the Christian peoples weep, bowed in sorrow. He was the father of all orphans, pilgrims, widows, and virgins. The kingdom of the Franks has suffered many disasters but never has it suffered such great grief as in that moment when the awe-inspiring and eloquent Charlemagne was laid to rest at Aachen. O Christ, welcome the pious Charlemagne into your blessed home among your apostles." This is how one monk at Bobbio put his sadness into words.

Einhard dedicated an entire chapter to the portents that announced Charlemagne's death and thereby emphasized that Charlemagne's importance extended far beyond that of other contemporaries. By the middle of the ninth century, Charlemagne appeared in a catalogue of martyrs—a calendar of the saints.

If Einhard's account was generally based on an idealized but still mostly true-to-life description of the great Frankish ruler, as early as 883, Notker Balbulus sketched a truly fantastic portrait in his *Gesta Karoli*, his *Deeds of Charles*. This work was dedicated to Charlemagne's great-grandson Charles III who had re-unified the empire of his great-grandfather. Notker made use of popular accounts concerning Charlemagne's life and deeds, but strove in addition to afford Charlemagne his appropriate place in world history. A form of historical writing current in the Middle Ages involved the model of the four successive worldly kingdoms which can be traced back to the well-known prophecy of Daniel. The last of these kingdoms was Rome. But with Charlemagne and the Frankish kingdom a new sequence began. Nevertheless, despite the glorification of Charles in this text, Notker doesn't call him "the Great." Indeed, his contemporaries never used this epithet to refer to the person of Charlemagne, but only in connection with his titles: "the great king," and later "the great emperor." It was only in the tenth and eleventh century that the epithet "the great" was used in historical works to describe the historical person Charlemagne.

Despite Notker's programmatic and idealized work, Charlemagne did not play an important role as a model or revered ancestor for the first Ottonian rulers. Admittedly, Otto the Great was crowned at Aachen in 936. However, Widukind of Corvey, our source, avoids mentioning the great Carolingian in this context. Nevertheless, the choice of Aachen as coronation site clearly points to Charlemagne, as does the presence of his crown and sword in the imperial treasury of the German kings and emperors. Otto himself certainly followed intentionally in Charlemagne's footsteps with his Italian policies and his own imperial coronation in 962. From that point on, the glorification of Charlemagne and the mythical aura associated with him continued to intensify. Otto III undertook a pilgrimage to Charlemagne's final resting place. After a long search, the grave was allegedly discovered. Otto had it opened and went inside, where he is supposed to have found the dead Charlemagne sitting on a throne. Just as strange as the alleged posture of the dead man was Otto's subsequent behavior. He cut off the finger nails of the corpse, which had bored through the armrests, he broke out a tooth to take away as a relic, and had the missing tip of the dead man's nose replaced with gold. It is quite possible that at the time Otto planned to have Charlemagne canonized since the search for a holy grave and fantastical details concerning the opening of the grave usually paved the way for canonization.

Otto III's behavior may be dismissed as simply the action of one individual, but another phenomenon demonstrates how widely the myth of Charlemagne had spread during the eleventh and twelfth centuries: numerous documents were forged in his name. Of the 262 surviving charters attributed to Charlemagne, 98, i.e. far more than one quarter, are forgeries. Most of the forgeries were produced during the twelfth century. Every monastery tried to outdo others by claiming that it had been granted a donation or confirmation of a privilege by the great emperor. Other kings and emperors were not as favored by the forgers, not even Otto the Great. This was also connected to the fact that most of the forgeries were produced in the context of legal conflicts in which older rights, and thus older privileges, were valued more than those of more recent origin. In terms of mythologizing, already apparent in Notker, Charlemagne undisputedly ranks highest among all the Germanic kings and emperors: over 1,000 legends are known about him. By contrast, there are little more than 50 concerning Barbarossa and only about 20 relating to Otto the Great.

Charlemagne's popularity among subsequent generations is certainly due, among other reason, to the fact that from the twelfth century onwards he was portrayed as a crusader and even as a saint. But the roots of this stylized portrayal reach even further back. Already in the tenth century, Andreas of Monte Soratte reported that Charlemagne had made a pilgrimage to Constantinople and Jerusalem. At the beginning of the twelfth century, that is after the First Crusade, a monk from Saint-Denis wrote an account of Charlemagne's crusade. With these legends, both monks wanted to explain how important relics had come to be in their monasteries: the bones of the sainted apostle Andrew in the case of Monte Soratte and the nail and Christ's crown of thorns at Saint-Denis.

During the course of the twelfth century, devotion to the myth of Charlemagne also increased in the western successor kingdom, France. The Old French *Chanson de Roland* (*The Song of Roland*), which dealt with Charlemagne's unsuccessful campaign against the Saracens in Spain in 778, originated during this time. In this campaign the rearguard of the Frankish army was annihilated by the Basques near Roncesvalles on its retreat through the gorges of the Pyrenees. *The Song of Roland* portrayed this defeat as a heroic and glorious battle of Christian knights against a superior infidel force. Roland and his companions fell as martyrs for their faith. By contrast, Charlemagne himself appears as a marginal figure whose great qualities are nevertheless emphasized. This account of a battle long past fit well with the mentality of the crusading period. *The Song of Roland* impressed contemporaries and mobilized fighters against Islam in Spain and in the Holy Land. But in the epic poem rising French national consciousness found expression, since Charlemagne was seen as a great French ruler. In Germany the translation by the cleric Conrad served to spread *The Song of Roland*. Charlemagne was presented as the ideal king not only in *The Song of Roland* but also in numerous other works of courtly literature.

In the twelfth century French veneration of Charlemagne focused on the Oriflamme, a shimmering red and gold banner. According to *The Song of Roland* the emperor had received it from the pope. Another legend recounted that the flag was the banner of Saint Dionysius, apostle of the city of Paris. It was for this reason that the banner was kept in the monastery church of Saint-Denis. When Emperor Henry V invaded France in 1124, King Louis VI followed the advice of Abbot Suger of Saint-Denis by having the Oriflamme carried in front of the French army. The retreat of the German emperor, before even facing battle, was ascribed to Charlemagne and Saint Dionysius. This success gave new impetus to the veneration of the great Carolingian in France. When Philip II, both of whose parents were descended from Charlemagne, came to the throne in 1180, this was celebrated as *reditus regni Francorum ad stirpem Caroli*, the return of the Frankish kingdom to the House of Charlemagne. It was Philip, with the significant epithet of Augustus, who was responsible for the ascendancy of France. In 1215, he defeated King John of England and the German emperor

Otto IV at the battle of Bouvines. From this point on, the French king claimed to be the true successor of Charlemagne. In order to imitate the twelve paladins who were supposed to have been present at Charlemagne's court, the king of France surrounded himself with twelve peers, his most powerful crown vassals. A sword that had long been kept in Saint-Denis and which was reputed to have belonged to Charlemagne was found. It soon became part of the royal insignia of the French kings. However, it was not only Charlemagne, but also the Merovingian kings Dagobert I and Clovis, the founder of the Frankish, and according to contemporary understanding, the French kingdom who were recalled.

No less important was the chronicle of the so-called Pseudo-Turpin supposedly written by Archbishop Turpin of Rheims, a contemporary of Charlemagne. This "witness" stood for the alleged authenticity of the work, which achieved an even wider circulation than the *Vita* by Einhard. This chronicle blended ecclesiastical–legendary traits with elements of folktales. Also fitting in with the twelfth century, Charlemagne was credited with having made a pilgrimage to Santiago de Compostella in northwestern Spain, which experienced an upturn as a pilgrimage site during this period. Along with his twelve paladins, as told in *The Song of Roland*, he is supposed to have visited the grave of the holy apostle James, with numerous miracles occurring along the way. Charlemagne's physical appearance was exaggerated to superhuman proportions. He was said to have been 8 feet tall, his face one and half spans long (one span = 25 cm), his beard one span, his nose half a span, and his eyebrows half a span. His forehead was said to be a foot wide, and his belt was supposedly eight spans long. Appropriate to his dimensions he consumed enormous amounts of meat. His strength was so great that he could lift an armed knight over his head from the floor with one hand or bend four horseshoes at once.

The first half of the twelfth century saw the development of numerous legends about Charlemagne in Germany as well, which indicates that here, too, conscious reference to the past and to the Frankish ruler intensified. The deeds of the great emperor were not only dealt with in Conrad's *Rolandslied*, but also in the "Imperial Chronicle" composed in Regensburg around 1150. That Emperor Frederick Barbarossa had Charlemagne canonized in 1165 was answer to the efforts of the French kings to monopolize the Frank for themselves. In order to justify this canonization, a monk from Aachen composed a further *vita Karoli magni* which was based primarily on legend not fact. Fifty years after Charlemagne's canonization, Barbarossa's grandson Frederick II had Charlemagne's bones placed in a newly built gold and silver casket. It was only from this point that the cult of the holy emperor achieved wider acceptance in the empire and then spread into France during the fourteenth and fifteenth centuries.

During the later Middle Ages, Charlemagne was regarded not only as a saint and a crusader but, especially in Germany, as the ideal lawgiver, and further as the founder of numerous institutions, the universities, the college of electors, the German episcopal constitution, and the counties. During the second half of the fourteenth century, Emperor Charles IV strove to intensify the veneration of his namesake in order to cultivate imperial traditions. Significantly, his nephew Charles V of France emulated him in order to strengthen his kingdom internally. He dubbed Charlemagne the patron saint of France and introduced the Charlemagne cult at his court. The veneration of Charlemagne in France reached its pinnacle during the second half of the fifteenth century. At the same time, it became increasingly instrumentalized in the context of steadily growing national consciousness in France. King Louis XI ordered the veneration of the holy emperor under penalty of death and tried to transform it into a kind of state religion. During Franco–German tensions at the end of the fifteenth century, Maximilian I for his part made much of his descent from Charlemagne in competition with the kings of France.

The dispute over the "nationality" of Charlemagne for the first time caused a special problem for study of him. It is in this context that historical sources were made available to a wider audience. In 1521, the cathedral provost of Cologne, Hermann Graf Neuenahr, had the *Vita* of Einhard and the royal annals printed for the first time. This edition was dedicated to Maximilian's grandson, Charles V, whom Neuenahr urged to imitate his namesake in fighting against his western neighbors. He naturally viewed Charlemagne as a German. This point had already been made as early as 1495 by the historian and abbot Johannes Trithemius. He gave as his reasons the fact that Charlemagne was born at Ingelheim, and that his mother tongue was German. Johann Wimpfeling from Schlettstadt shared this view and even expanded it: Charlemagne was the first German emperor, and he carried out his most important actions on German soil. Thomas Murner, a Franciscan popular preacher from Alsace, expressed a more moderate view. He stressed that Charlemagne was *Gallus atque Germanus*, both French and German, and that he had supported equally all peoples of his empire. The dominant position remained, however, the instrumental claim for humanist patriotism: the Bavarian chronicler Johannes Turmair, called Aventinus, declared that Charlemagne was a Bavarian who had been born in Karlsburg (near Munich).

In Italy, references of this type to Charlemagne were viewed more skeptically. There, people were more reluctant in their judgments of the Frankish ruler because the Renaissance provided greater models. A comparison of his achievements with the successes of the ancient Roman emperors could only be to Charlemagne's detriment. Nevertheless, from time to time in Italy he was also regarded as an ideal ruler, as the renewer of the imperial dignity, and as the protector of town privileges. His pilgrimages, however, were banished into the realm of fantasy. Source criticism thus became mixed with the widespread need to explain and to solve problems using the past. Machiavelli did not include Charlemagne in his list of model princes—that is to say among those who pursued their political agendas without scruples—because Charlemagne had received the imperial dignity from the pope instead of sitting in judgment on him. Thus, the superiority of the papacy over the empire was traced back to the Carolingians.

After the Reformation, a further component was added to the continuing widespread idealization of Charlemagne in legends and his use for national goals: he was referred to in confessional struggles, despite the fact that after 1568 he was no longer included in the official list of Catholic saints. In 1549, the *Libri Carolini* were printed. Only a year later, Calvin quoted them in an effort to provide a historical basis for the reformist rejection of the veneration of icons. By contrast, the Catholics sought in vain to prove the *Libri Carolini* a forgery. During the sixteenth and seventeenth centuries, the Protestants, especially, stressed the conflict between the Frankish ruler and the papacy. In considering problems related to the veneration of relics, celibacy, or the judgment of the papacy Charlemagne was considered to be a forerunner of the Reformation. Yet Luther criticized

Charlemagne because he had accepted the empire from the papacy. Over the course of the sixteenth century, scholarly interest in Charlemagne's rule grew. The capitularies were edited and gave an impression of Charlemagne's extensive activities as a ruler. The Maurist monk Jean Mabillon subjected Charlemagne's charters to strict source criticism. In addition, he fixed Charlemagne's birth date as 742 and birthplace at Aachen ignoring petty nationalist jealousies. In 1677, Etienne Baluze published the first critical edition of the capitularies.

The discussions and arguments about Charlemagne became increasingly scholarly but not necessarily more objective. The religiously tinged historiography of the sixteenth and seventeenth centuries generally approved of the execution of 4,500 Saxons at Verden on the Aller. Leibniz, however, who was in the service of the Elector of Hanover, followed enlightenment traditions in condemning this event as a barbaric act which cast a shadow over Charlemagne's otherwise positive achievements. Montesquieu saw in Charlemagne the first constitutional ruler and—befitting his own interests—emphasized Charlemagne's concern for the freemen whose oppression by the nobles he sought to alleviate. Voltaire, who gathered together all the previously disparate criticisms, disapproved passionately of Charlemagne: his state church, his despotism, which was most obvious at Verden, and his polygamy. He could not even write his own name and yet had gone down in history as the supporter of scholarship. This thousandfold murderer was declared a saint by the church. In Voltaire's view, Charlemagne was a typical representative of an age, which Voltaire perceived as dark, especially because of what he considered its barbaric ordering of society, the careless association of state with religion, of policies with dogma, of slavery with Christianity. His Muslim contemporary

Harun-al-Rashid thoroughly surpassed him in justice, education, and humanity, according to Voltaire. This attack was directed primarily at the legitimacy of the French monarchy of his own time which still drew on its connection to Charlemagne. But the myth of the Frankish ruler survived. Even in 1804 Napoleon visited Charlemagne's crypt at Aachen and two years later wrote to the pope, "Je suis Charlemagne." More than a few of his contemporaries referred to him as "Charlemagne reborn."

In Germany at the same time, the shortcomings of Charlemagne and his reign were also noticed. But in an era of increasing national consciousness, the Carolingian epoch offered an important point of reference. Justus Möser stressed in 1768 that many institutions of his time had their origins under Charlemagne. This epoch was imagined as a golden age marked by the existence of free farmers. The German writer Herder shared this view but also stressed that Charlemagne passed on to succeeding generations what he had sought to suppress, namely vassality, the system of estates, as well as narrow-minded monastic schools and cathedral chapters. He even inwardly rejected the imperial dignity. Moreover, Charlemagne proved to be too great for his successors who were unable to maintain what he had achieved. Other contemporaries did not share this enthusiasm for Charlemagne and the "democratic, grassroots" constitution of his empire. The poet Karl Ludwig von Woltmann cherished the hope that Napoleon, as the legitimate successor of the Frankish emperor, would not repeat these errors.

The Romantics admired Charlemagne almost without reservation. According to Friedrich Schlegel, Charlemagne was "the lawgiver for the whole of western Europe." It was only Charlemagne's efforts on behalf of the German language which fell short, and the brutality of his Saxon mission, which could not be swept under the rug. During the Wars of Liberation, Charlemagne came to be seen as the founder the Germanic nation and of the Holy Roman Empire of the German Nation that ceased to exist in 1806 and which gradually came to be part of the Romantic idealized view of the medieval past. The poets Grimm and Uhland collected numerous tales about the first Frankish emperor. Historians also intensified their studies of the sources relevant to the Carolingian era. The *Monumenta Germaniae Historica*, the first volume of which appeared in 1826, was devoted to historical sources of the Carolingian period; it was started through the influence of the former Prussian minister Freiherr vom Stein. Just as the basis for further scholarly research of Charlemagne was established, rising nationalism became less and less connected to him. Certainly, he was credited with a contribution to the foundations of the German nation, but at the same time, as already noted, he was seen as the "butcher" of the Saxons. Moreover, he did not renew "Germanic liberties." Instead, he prepared the way for feudalism. The critical distance went so far that his Frankish origins were denied and he was transformed into a "Romantic." As a result, Charlemagne could not become "the timeless symbol of the German nation." (A. Borst)

A similar pattern emerged in France. Napoleon's cult of Charlemagne ended with his fall. Discussions about Charlemagne's achievements still focused on his rule, although his cultural efforts came more and more into view. He was seen as the renewer of Roman civilization. It was in this context that in 1840 the Parisian literary historian Jean-Jacques-Antoine Ampère used the word "renaissance." The actual points of reference for this admiration were not, however, Charlemagne himself and his time but rather classical antiquity, especially the Roman world. Consequently, his contribution was no longer a suitable basis for regarding Charlemagne as a pioneer of the French nation. The more discussion of Charlemagne avoided contemporary problems the more he became the object of specialized historical studies, even if research was not completely divorced from contemporary concerns as indicated by the views of individual historians.

The great nineteenth-century German historian Leopold von Ranke regarded Charlemagne's empire, which encompassed most of Western Europe, as the common root of European nations. His student Wilhelm von Giesebrecht, for his part, contrasted the fragmentation of Germany around 1850 with the power and stability of Charlemagne's medieval empire. Heinrich von Sybel, another of Ranke's students, opposed this view: the Italian and imperial policies were seen as mistakes that in the end overstretched the strength of the young German nation. By contrast, the historian Julius Ficker applauded the expansion to the south. This dispute among scholars was dominated by the problem of the historically determined fate of the German nation. Georg Waitz, yet another of Ranke's students, warned against placing too much emphasis on the current state of the nation. Charlemagne had done no more than prepare the way for German history by uniting and converting to Christianity the German tribes.

The rising nationalism following the unification of Germany in 1871 once more brought attention to one of Charlemagne's deeds that did not seem to fit the atmosphere of the period, namely the bloodbath at Verden. An effort was made to exonerate the Frankish ruler of this deed. And the cynical argument was put forward that even this incomparable act of revenge could not diminish Charlemagne's greatness. Apart from this, around 1900, scholarly interest centered on the question of whether or not Charlemagne had followed some master plan. Here too, the national question stood in the foreground. Did Charlemagne act as a Germanic war king or did he follow the example of the Byzantine state? Was he simply a king of the Frankish people or was he a Germanic Caesar?

During the Nazi era, there was yet again an emphasis on the question of the bloodbath at Verden. Charlemagne was the "butcher of the Saxons" who forgot his Germanic origins and, while pursuing the alien Christian religion, brutally subjugated the racially related Saxons. A debate concerning Charlemagne's Germanic identity ensued which was halted by Hitler himself. He expressly forbade Charlemagne to be described as the "butcher of the Saxons." In the end, Charlemagne had established a large Germanic empire which served as a model for Hitler's own overarching ambitions, and which was an express source of inspiration for his idea of the "Third Reich." During World War II, romance-speaking members of the SS served the *Reich* in a division named "Charlemagne."

The discussion of Charlemagne's nationality ended after 1945. Instead, he became the "Father of Europe." Since 1950, the city of Aachen has given the *Karlspreis* (Charlemagne Prize) to those individuals who have contributed to the unification of Europe. Thus, in 1965, the 800th anniversary of Charlemagne's canonization was marked by a large exhibition in Aachen which was held under the auspices of the Council of Europe. The introduction to the exhibition catalogue noted explicitly the fact that the territory of Charlemagne's empire corresponded, "largely with the current European Economic Community." Furthermore, the most recent exhibition concerning the (Merovingian)

Franks at Mannheim, Berlin, and Paris in 1996 was held under the motto of the historical roots of Europe. Thus, modern scholarship strives in such public forums to draw a clear distinction between past and present. As early as 1949, the medievalist Heinrich Fichtenau warned against too strong an idealization of Charlemagne. He pursued great goals, but in the end he failed, even in his efforts to secure the inner unity of his large empire. Fundamentally, caution is always justified when the past is used to justify present conditions or goals. The best possible study of Charlemagne's history is one free of preconceptions.

Chronology

Chronology

741	Death of Charles Martel; Carloman and Pippin the Younger eliminate their half-brother Grifo
743	Carloman and Pippin put the Merovingian Childeric III on the throne
747	Carloman abdicates
748	2 April, birth of Charlemagne
751	Pippin crowned king
754	Pope Stephen II travels to Francia; Pippin's first campaign against the Lombards
756	Pippin's second campaign against the Lombards
760–768	Conquest of Aquitaine
768	Death of Pippin; his successors are his sons Charlemagne and Carloman
771	Death of Carloman; Charlemagne becomes sole ruler
772	First campaign against the Saxons; Destruction of the Irminsul
773/74	Conquest of the Lombard kingdom, first expedition to Rome
775–780	Campaigns against the Saxons
778	Campaign to Spain
781	Second expedition to Rome; Charlemagne's sons Pippin and Louis are anointed and crowned by Pope Hadrian
782	Saxon revolt under Widukind, Battle of Süntel; bloodbath at Verden on the Aller, *Capitulatio de partibus Saxoniae*

Chronology

783–785	Renewed subjugation of the Saxons
785	Baptism of Widukind at Attigny
787	Third expedition to Rome, campaign against Arichis of Benevento, campaign against Duke Tassilo III of Bavaria who becomes Charlemagne's vassal; Council of Nicaea
788	Trial of Tassilo in Ingelheim
789	*Admonitio generalis*, the first general oath
791	First campaign against the Avars
792–799	Renewed revolts in Saxony
792/93	Revolt of Pippin the Hunchback against his father Charlemagne
794	Synod of Frankfurt
795/96	Successful campaigns against the Avars under Margrave Eric of Friuli and King Pippin of Italy
797	*Capitulare Saxonicum*
799	Pope Leo III flees from his Roman opponents to Charlemagne at Paderborn
800	Fourth journey to Rome; the imperial coronation of Charlemagne on 25th of December in St. Peter's Basilica
802	Imperial assembly at Aachen, issuing of important reform capitularies, the second general oath
804	Last Saxon campaign
806	*Divisio regnorum*

Chronology

Suggestions for Further Reading

Compiled by Jennifer Davis

The bibliography on Charlemagne is immense. The following list is a selection among the many relevant studies, emphasizing scholarship in English. The works noted here offer a few ways into the long and varied tradition of historiography on Charlemagne and the Carolingians.

General Works on the Carolingians

Abel, S. finished by B. von Simson. *Jahrbücher des fränkischen Reiches unter Karl dem Grossen.* 2nd. ed. 2 vols. Reprinted Berlin, 1969.

Böhmer, J.F. and E. Mühlbacher, completed by J. Lechner with L. Santifaller, with a foreword and tables by C. Brühl and H.H. Kaminsky. *Regesta Imperii.* Vol. 1: *Die Regesten des Kaiserreichs unter den Karolingern 751–918.* Hildesheim, 1966.

Bullough, D.A. *The Age of Charlemagne.* 2nd. ed. London, 1973.

Suggestions for Further Reading

Bullough, D.A. "*Europae Pater*: Charlemagne and his Achievement in the Light of Recent Scholarship," *English Historical Review* 85 (1970), 59–105.

Fichtenau, H. *The Carolingian Empire*. Trans. P. Munz. Medieval Academy Reprints for Teaching 1. Toronto, 1978.

Die Franken: Wegbereiter Europas. Vor 1500 Jahren: König Chlodwig und seine Erben. 2 vols. Mainz, 1996.

Halphen, L. *Charlemagne and the Carolingian Empire*. Trans. G. de Nie. Europe in the Middle Ages 3. Amsterdam, New York, and Oxford, 1977.

Karl der Grosse: Lebenswerk und Nachleben. Ed. W. Braunfels. 5 vols. Düsseldorf, 1965–1968.

McKitterick, R. *The Frankish Kingdoms under the Carolingians, 751–987*. London, 1983.

The New Cambridge Medieval History. Vol. 2. Ed. R. McKitterick. Cambridge, 1995.

Riché, P. *The Carolingians: A Family Who Forged Europe*. Trans. M.I. Allen. The Middle Ages Series. Philadelphia, 1993.

Riché, P. *Daily Life in the World of Charlemagne*. Trans. J. McNamara. The Middle Ages Series. Philadelphia, 1978.

Schieffer, R. *Die Karolinger*. Stuttgart, 1992.

Sullivan, R.E. "The Carolingian Age: Reflections on its Place in the History of the Middle Ages," *Speculum* 64 (1989), 267–306.

Suggestions for Further Reading

Primary Source Collections and Translations

Carolingian Chronicles. Trans. B.W. Scholz with B. Rogers. Ann Arbor, 1970.

Carolingian Civilization: A Reader. Ed. P. E. Dutton. Peterborough, Ontario, 1993.

Charlemagne: Translated Sources. Trans. P.D. King. Lancaster, 1987.

Charlemagne's Courtier: The Complete Einhard. Ed. and trans. P.E. Dutton. Readings in Medieval Civilizations and Cultures 2. Peterborough, Ontario, 1998.

Fredegar. *Chronicon.* Ed. and trans. J.M. Wallace-Hadrill as *The Fourth Book of the Chronicle of Fredegar, with its continuations.* Connecticut, 1960.

Late Merovingian France: History and Hagiography 640–720. Trans. P. Fouracre and R.A. Gerberding. Manchester Medieval Sources Series. Manchester, 1996.

Poetry of the Carolingian Renaissance. Ed. and trans. P. Godman. Norman, Oklahoma, 1985.

The Reign of Charlemagne: Documents on Carolingian Government and Administration. Trans. H.R. Loyn and J. Percival. Documents of Medieval History 2. London, 1975.

Two Lives of Charlemagne. Trans. L. Thorpe. London, 1969.

Chapter 1

799, Kunst und Kultur der Karolingerzeit: Karl der Grosse und Papst Leo III. in Paderborn: Beiträge zum Katalog der Ausstellung, Paderborn, 1999. Ed. C. Stiegemann and M. Wemhoff. 2 vols. Mainz, 1999.

Suggestions for Further Reading

Am Vorabend der Kaiserkrönung. Das Epos „Karolus Magnus et Leo Papa" und der Papstbesuch in Paderborn. Ed. J. Jarnut, P. Godman, and P. Johanek. Paderborn, 2002.

Becher, M. "Die Kaiserkrönung im Jahr 800. Eine Streitfrage zwishen Karl dem Grossen und Papst Leo III." *Rheinische Vierteljahrsblätter* 66 (2002), 1–38.

Classen, P. *Karl der Grosse, das Papsttum und Byzanz: Die Begründung des karolingischen Kaisertums.* Ed. H. Fuhrmann and K. Märtl. Beiträge zur Geschichte und Quellenkunde des Mittelalters 9. Sigmaringen, 1985.

The Coronation of Charlemagne: What Did it Signify? Ed. R.E. Sullivan. Problems in European Civilization. Boston, 1959.

Folz, R. *The Coronation of Charlemagne 25 December 800.* Trans. J.E. Anderson. London, 1974.

Fried, J. "Papst Leo III. besucht Karl den Grossen in Paderborn oder Einhards Schweigen," *Historische Zeitschrift* 272 (2001), 281–326.

Ganshof, F.L. *The Imperial Coronation of Charlemagne: Theories and Facts.* Glasgow University Publications 79. Glasgow, 1949.

Mayr-Harting, H. "Charlemagne, the Saxons, and the Imperial Coronation of 800," *English Historical Review* 111 (1996), 1113–33.

Ullmann, W. *The Carolingian Renaissance and the Idea of Kingship.* Birkbeck Lectures, 1968–1969. London, 1969.

Chapter 2

Becher, M. "Neue Überlegungen zum Geburtsdatum Karls des Grossen," *Francia* 19 (1992), 37–60.

Suggestions for Further Reading

Fouracre, P. *The Age of Charles Martel*. The Medieval World. Harlow, England and New York, 2000.

Fried, J. *Der Weg in die Geschichte. Die Ursprünge Deutschlands bis 1024*. Propyläen Geschichte Deutschlands 1. Berlin, 1994.

Geary, P. *Before France and Germany: The Creation and Transformation of the Merovingian World*. New York and Oxford, 1988.

James, E. *The Origins of France from Clovis to the Capetians 500–1000*. New Studies in Medieval History. London, 1982.

Karl Martell in seiner Zeit. Ed. J. Jarnut, U. Nonn, M. Richter with M. Becher and W. Reinsch. Beihefte der Francia 37. Sigmaringen, 1994.

Wood, I. *The Merovingian Kingdoms 450–751*. London, 1994.

Chapter 3

Angenendt, A. "Das geistliche Bündnis der Päpste mit den Karolingern (754–796)," *Historisches Jahrbuch* 100 (1980), 1–94.

Early Medieval Rome and the Christian West: Essays in Honour of Donald A. Bullough. Ed. J.M.H. Smith. The Medieval Mediterranean: Peoples, Economies and Cultures, 400–1453, 28. Leiden, Boston, and Cologne, 2000.

Hannig, J. *Consensus fidelium: Frühfeudale Interpretationen des Verhältnisses von Königtum und Adel am Beispiel des Frankenreiches*. Monographien zur Geschichte des Mittelalters 27. Stuttgart, 1982.

Jarnut, J. "Ein Bruderkampf und seine Folgen: Die Krise des Frankenreiches (768–771)," in *Herrschaft, Kirche, Kultur: Beiträge zur Geschichte des Mittelalters. Festschrift für Friedrich Prinz zu seinem 65. Geburtstag*. Ed. G. Jenal with S. Haarländer. Monographien zur Geschichte des Mittelalters 37. Stuttgart, 1993, 165–76.

Nelson, J.L. "Making a Difference in Eighth-Century Politics: The Daughters of Desiderius," in *After Rome's Fall: Narrators and Sources of Early Medieval History. Essays presented to Walter Goffart*. Ed. A.C. Murray. Toronto, 1998, 171–90.

Richter, M. "Die „lange Machtergreifung" der Karolinger. Der Staatsstreich gegen die Merowinger in den Jahren 747–771," in *Grosse Verschwörungen. Staatsstreich und Tyrannensturz von der Antike bis zur Gegenwart*. Ed. U. Schulze. Munich, 1998, 48–59.

Schmid, K. "Zur Ablösung der Langobardenherrschaft durch die Franken," in his *Gebetsgedenken und adliges Selbstverständnis im Mittelalter: Ausgewählte Beiträge. Festgabe zu seinem sechzigsten Geburtstag*. Ed. G. Althoff and D. Geuenich. Sigmaringen, 1983, 268–303.

Tabacco, G. *The Struggle for Power in Medieval Italy. Structures of Political Rule*. Trans. R. Brown Jensen. Cambridge Medieval Textbooks. Cambridge, 1989.

Chapter 4

Airlie, S. "Narratives of Triumph and Rituals of Submission: Charlemagne's Mastering of Bavaria," *Transactions of the Royal Historical Society* 6th series 9 (1999), 93–119.

Die Bajuwaren von Severin bis Tassilo 488–788. Ed. H. Dannheimer et. al. Munich, 1988.

Becher, M. "*Non enim habent regem idem Antiqui Saxones* . . . Verfassung und Ethnogenese in Sachsen während des 8. Jahrhunderts," in *Sachsen und Franken in Westfalen. Zur Komplexität der ethnischen Deutung und Abgrenzung zweier frühmittelalterlicher Stämme*. Studien zur Sachsenforschung 12. Oldenburg, 1999, 1–31.

Suggestions for Further Reading

Bowlus, C.R. *Franks, Moravians, and Magyars: The Struggle for the Middle Danube, 788–907*. The Middle Ages Series. Philadelphia, 1995.

Brown, W. *Unjust Seizure: Conflict, Interest, and Authority in an Early Medieval Society*. Conjunctions of Religion and Power in the Medieval Past. Ithaca and London, 2001.

Innes, M. "Franks and Slavs c.700–1000: The Problem of European Expansion Before the Millennium," *Early Medieval Europe* 6 (1997), 201–216.

Kahl, H.-D. "Karl der Grosse und die Sachsen. Stufen und Motive einer historischen „Eskalation"," in *Politik, Gesellschaft, Geschichtsschreibung. Giessener Festgabe für František Graus zum 60. Geburtstag*. Ed. H. Ludat and R.C. Schwinges. Beihefte zum Archiv für Kulturgeschichte 18. Cologne and Vienna, 1982, 49–130.

Leyser, K.J. *Rule and Conflict in an Early Medieval Society: Ottonian Saxony*. Oxford, 1989.

Pearson, K.L.R. *Conflicting Loyalties in Early Medieval Bavaria: A View of Socio-Political Interaction, 680–900*. Aldershot, 1999.

Pohl, W. *Die Awaren. Ein Steppenvolk in Mitteleuropa 567–827 n. Chr.* Frühe Völker. Munich, 1988.

Reuter, T. "Plunder and Tribute in the Carolingian Empire," *Transactions of the Royal Historical Society* 5th series 35 (1985), 75–94.

Schubert, E. "Die *Capitulatio de partibus Saxoniae*," in *Geschichte in der Region. Zum 65. Geburtstag von Heinrich Schmidt*. Ed. D. Brosius, et. al. Veröffentlichungen der historischen Kommission für Niedersachsen und Bremen Sonderband. Hanover, 1993, 3–28.

Caspar, E. *Das Papsttum unter fränkischer Herrschaft.* Darmstadt, 1956.

Das Frankfurter Konzil von 794: Kristallisationspunkt Karolingischer Kultur. Ed. R. Berndt. 2 vols. Quellen und Abhandlungen zur mittelrheinischen Kirchengeschichte 80. Mainz, 1997.

Freeman, A. "Carolingian Orthodoxy and the Fate of the *Libri Carolini*," *Viator* 16 (1985), 65–108.

Grierson, P. "The Coronation of Charlemagne and the Coinage of Pope Leo III," *Revue belge de philologie et d'histoire* 30 (1952), 825–33.

Hlawitschka, E. *Franken, Alemannen, Bayern und Burgunder in Oberitalien (774–962).* Forschungen zur oberrheinischen Landesgeschichte 8. Freiburg, 1960.

McCormick, M. "Diplomacy and the Carolingian Encounter with Byzantium down to the Accession of Charles the Bald," in *Eriugena: East and West. Papers of the Eighth International Colloquium of the Society for the Promotion of Eriugenian Studies.* Ed. B. McGinn and W. Otten. Notre Dame Conferences in Medieval Studies 5. Notre Dame and London, 1994, 15–48.

McCormick, M. "Textes, images et iconoclasme dans le cadre des relations entre Byzance et l'Occident carolingien," in *Testo e Immagine nell'alto Medioevo.* Settimane di studio del centro Italiano di studi sull'alto Medioevo 41. Spoleto, 1994, 95–158.

Noble, T.F.X. *The Republic of St. Peter: The Birth of the Papal State, 680–825.* The Middle Ages Series. Philadelphia, 1984.

Noble, T.F.X. "Topography, Celebration, and Power: The Making of a Papal Rome in the Eighth and Ninth Centuries," in *Topographies of*

Power in the Early Middle Ages. Ed. M. de Jong and F. Theuws, with C. van Rhijn. Transformations of the Roman World 6. Leiden, Boston, and Cologne, 2001, 45–91.

Wickham, C. *Early Medieval Italy: Central Power and Local Society 400–1000.* London, 1981.

Chapter 6

Becher, M. *Eid und Herrschaft: Untersuchungen zum Herrscherethos Karls des Grossen.* Vorträge und Forschungen (Konstanzer Arbeitskreis für mittelalterliche Geschichte) 39. Sigmaringen, 1993.

Bullough, Donald. "*Aula Renovata*: The Carolingian Court Before the Aachen Palace," *Proceedings of the British Academy* 71 (1985), 267–301.

de Clercq, C. *La législation religieuse franque de Clovis à Charlemagne: étude sur les actes de conciles et les capitulaires, les statuts diocésians et les règles monastiques (507–814).* Vol. 1. Recueil de travaux publiés par les membres des Conférances d'histoire et de philologie 2ᵉ série, 38. Paris and Louvain, 1936.

Eckhardt, W.A. "Die *Capitularia missorum specialia* 802," *Deutsches Archiv* 12 (1956), 498–516.

Fouracre, P. "Carolingian Justice: The Rhetoric of Improvement and Contexts of Abuse," in *La Giustizia nell'alto Medioevo (secoli V–VIII).* Settimane di studio del centro Italiano di studi sull'alto Medioevo 42. Spoleto, 1995, 771–803.

Ganshof, F.L. *The Carolingians and the Frankish Monarchy: Studies in Carolingian History.* Trans. J. Sondheimer. London, 1971.

Ganshof, F.L. *Recherches sur les capitulaires.* Paris, 1958.

Suggestions for Further Reading

McKitterick, R. *The Frankish Church and the Carolingian Reforms, 789–895.* London, 1977.

Nelson, J.L. "Kingship and Royal Government," in the *New Cambridge Medieval History.* Vol. 2. Ed. R. McKitterick. Cambridge, 1995, 383–430.

Noble, T.F.X. "From Brigandage to Justice: Charlemagne, 785–794," in *Literacy, Politics, and Artistic Innovation in the Early Medieval West.* Ed. C.M. Chazelle. Lanham, New York, and London, 1992, 49–75.

Odegaard, C.E. "The Concept of Royal Power in Carolingian Oaths of Fidelity," *Speculum* 20 (1945), 279–289.

Werner, K.F. "Missus-marchio-comes. Entre l'administration centrale et l'administration locale de l'empire carolingien," in *Histoire comparée de l'administration.* Ed. W. Paravicini and K.F. Werner. Actes du XIVe colloque historique franco-allemand de l'Institut Historique Allemand de Paris. Beihefte der Francia 9. Munich, 1980, 191–239.

Chapter 7

Classen, P. "Karl der Grosse und die Thronfolge im Frankenreich," in *Festschrift für Hermann Heimpel zum 70. Geburtstag.* 3 vols. Veröffentlichungen des Max-Planck Instituts für Geschichte 36. Göttingen, 1972, vol. 3, 109–134.

Goffart, W. "Paul the Deacon's '*Gesta Episcoporum Mettensium*' and the Early Design of Charlemagne's Succession," *Traditio* 42 (1986), 59–93.

Innes, M. "Charlemagne's Will: Piety, Politics and the Imperial Succession," *English Historical Review* 112 (1997), 833–855.

Kasten, B. *Königssöhne und Königsherrschaft. Untersuchungen zur Teilhabe am Reich in der Merowinger- und Karolingerzeit.* Monumenta Germaniae Historica Schriften 44. Hanover, 1997.

Nelson, J.L. "La famille de Charlemagne," *Byzantion* 61 (1991), 194–212.

Nelson, J.L. "Women at the Court of Charlemagne: A Case of Monstrous Regiment?", in *Medieval Queenship.* Ed. J.C. Parsons. New York, 1993, 43–61.

The Uses of the Past in the Early Middle Ages. Ed. Y. Hen and M. Innes. Cambridge, 2000.

Zum Kaisertum Karls des Grossen. Beiträge und Aufsätze. Ed. G. Wolf. Wege der Forschung 38. Darmstadt, 1972.

Chapter 8

Airlie, S. "After Empire—Recent Work on the Emergence of Post-Carolingian Kingdoms," *Early Medieval Europe* 2 (1993), 153–161.

Boshof, E. *Ludwig der Fromme.* Darmstadt, 1996.

Charlemagne's Heir: New Perspectives on the Reign of Louis the Pious (814–840). Ed. R. Collins and P. Godman. Oxford, 1990.

Folz, R. *Le souvenir et la légende de Charlemagne dans l'Empire germanique médiéval.* Publications de l'université de Dijon 7. Paris, 1950.

Goldberg, E. "'More Devoted to the Equipment of Battle than the Splendor of Banquets': Frontier Kingship, Military Ritual and Early Knighthood at the Court of Louis the German," *Viator* 30 (1999), 41–78.

Suggestions for Further Reading

Karl der Grosse als vielberufener Vorfahr. Sein Bild in der Kunst der Fürsten, Kirchen und Städte. Ed. L.E. Saurma-Jeltsch. Schriften des historischen Museums 19. Sigmaringen, 1994.

Kerner, M. *Karl der Grosse. Entschleierung eines Mythos.* Cologne, Weimar, and Vienna, 2001.

Mühlner, H. *Die Sachsenkriege Karls des Grossen in der Geschichtsschreibung der Karolinger- und Ottonenzeit.* Historische Studien 308. Berlin, 1937.

Nelson, J.L. *Charles the Bald.* The Medieval World. London, 1992.

The New Cambridge Medieval History. Vol. 3. Ed. T. Reuter. Cambridge, 1999.

Werner, K.F. *Karl der Grosse oder Charlemagne? Von der Aktualität einer überholten Fragestellung.* Sitzungsberichte der Bayerischen Akademie der Wissenschaften, phil.-hist. Kl., Heft 4. Munich, 1995.

Index

Index

Index

Lightning Source UK Ltd.
Milton Keynes UK
UKOW04f1416031215

263972UK00001B/1/P